BLACK SHEEP CAUGHT IN A COBWEB

BLACK SHEEP CAUGHT IN A COBWEB
PART ONE

MIRABELLE PEREIRA

PARTRIDGE

ISBN:	Hardcover	978-1-4828-8586-6
	Softcover	978-1-4828-8585-9
	eBook	978-1-4828-8584-2

Print information available on the last page.

To order additional copies of this book, contact
Partridge India
000 800 10062 62
orders.india@partridgepublishing.com

www.partridgepublishing.com/india

Contents

Foreword

'Humour is the essence of life...'

I am glad that our young writer 'Mirabelle Pereira' has made a foray into story writing introducing humour as part of life's journey to happiness.

It is interesting that each anecdote ends with a smile giving a lovely twist to an otherwise regrettable end!

Keep it up- this is just a beginning to a glorious, humorous life!

Nana Chudasama

Preface

In the famous opening line of Russian classic *Anna Karenina*, Leo Tolstoy writes, *'All happy families are alike. Every unhappy family is unhappy in its own way.'*

I still haven't decided whether we are an unhappy or a happy family, but I do know that we are certainly not like any other on this planet. Watching a recent movie with my grandparents and mother (only half my family) was a surreal experience. Not only because it was an entertaining film, but also because it felt like watching a home video. There on screen was a dysfunctional family hiding their imperfections and insecurities for the sake of saving face in the upper class society they belonged to, only to finally lose it as there's only so long you can lie to yourself and the world. That was definitely us, except we hit our breaking point a long time back.

We are a group of oddballs. There is simply no better word to describe us. If you had to make a list of what one would view as dreaded or controversial, we've covered it—gold digging relatives, divorce, adoption, cancer . . . and those don't even cover it all. But this book won't discuss all of these. Whether people will view this as a posh person's angst or baseless writing, it is up to them. But the one thing

I can guarantee you that won't be said is, 'This happens in our family as well. These events are nothing special' because that's just not possible. Every family is mad in a different way.

What has stayed constant about my family is, despite going through all these ups, downs, turns, hurdles, and rollercoaster rides, we've never let go of our sense of humour. Laughing at the hilarity of our situation and saying, 'This could only happen to us,' not in a self-pitying but a self-deprecating fashion is a tradition this book celebrates. I've chosen twenty episodes stretching in chronological order reflecting on some of the most bizarre stories I have to tell.

We may be self-deprecating, but we aren't cynical about the future given our past together. Everything else in our lives has, can, and will vary but till date I am yet to see a unit that has remained as tightly knit as ours. I would like to believe that many more units like us exist. Most importantly, it is my sole prerogative to make fun of my family and laugh at them—everyone else is more than welcome to laugh with them.

All names have been changed to preserve the dignity of those involved. All incidents are 100 per cent true, including dialogues, characters, and details.

For you, Catherine, the stray kitten (R.I.P).

Introduction

Self-diagnosis:

The grandmother
- A pathological liar hosting secret blackjack meetings everyday at home which she dubs as a daily 'computer class'.

The grandfather
- Second in line to the matriarch, he often disappears on mysterious foreign trips and emerges when a whisky bottle is popped out despite having suffered from two strokes.

The mother
- Definitely suffering from social anxiety and nervous disorder; known for a beetroot-like complexion enhanced by her particularly thin layer of skin that allows you to see her veins and arteries. Never needs an x-ray.

Jasmine, the aunt
- A victim of hypomania where she has a chance to show off her virtuous self by taking on tasks too

ambitious for the shoes she's worn; her favourite being that of a tiger mother.

Keith, the uncle
- Hit hard by the truck of obesity but combating those results through regular marathons where he has a chance to show off his dragon tattoo.

Sid, the brother
- A love-sick boy, suffering from chronic laziness. Not much else is known about him.

Zara, the cousin
- All of seven years of age, having terrified three nannies back to their villages; she is known for her Mary Kom-esque build and regularly does 100 push ups on the bar.

Myself, Mirabelle
- Bitten by the bug of insanity from the time; I was born much like the rest of the gang, the effects of this are being revealed by the day.

Chapter 1

Nita 1.0

Sanity is a façade we put on for society; madness is the state we are put in by family.

I sat on my grandmother's bed as she spoke on the phone, 'Okay, yes, she'll be coming on Tuesday-yes, her mother will accompany her.' I had no idea where she wanted me to go, but I was already dreading it.

From the time I was five, I was told that I would attend 'talking classes'— a strange procedure in which I would go inside and talk about my feelings, as my mother sat patiently outside engrossed in a magazine. We would take turns to do this. Of course, it was only at the age of 12, three years after those classes had stopped, that I realised I had actually been seeing a shrink. I still don't know what was wrong with me.

My mother would accompany me every Wednesday during my summer break at 11.30 a.m. to meet with who was apparently the most accomplished psychiatrist in the country—Dr Nita. Her office undoubtedly did her justice as we trudged with extreme caution down three crumbling stairs to wait for the door to be graciously answered. We often stood for more than five minutes in the energy sapping heat, watching a bucket in the corner collect dripping water from a pipe stretching from a toilet whose existence I am still in denial about. When we were finally let in, I would walk inside the whitewashed walls of Nita's office and a few pleasant meetings ensued.

I really believe she treated our equation like a marriage, given that her true colours were only released after the seven-month itch. Polite, less intrusive questions like, 'What are your hobbies?' and 'Tell me about your friends' became 'Are you racist?' and 'Do you not like your brother because he's darker than you?' These all made great sense given that we hailed from the same subcontinent and I was by no means of a peaches-and-cream complexion; not that I wished to be otherwise at all.

The strangest incident has to be when after refusing her weekly offering of a beverage she asked, 'Does your religion not permit you to accept things I offer?' I was stumped not because I was offended, but because I wondered what religion she was that prevented her from understanding why one would refuse cheese and onion crackers at nine o'clock in the morning?

'No, it's okay' was my automatic answer to this as for most questions she asked. I was on autopilot for most meetings until she bid me goodbye and I made no bones about revealing my relief. Once, at a poignant moment of sorts, when she fumbled about on the computer struggling to remember her password, I stared at a certificate on the wall asserting her adequacy in providing help to those dealing with Alzheimer's. Strangely, the other side of her office housed an emblem of her faith. In this case, an idol of Jesus crucified with a candle lit below. At least, she was aware of the damage she was causing to all her patients and had the decency to pray for us. The only way to sum up the absurdity of her thought process is with one of the tumbler style quotes she had on one of the cards on her desk—'Mistakes are proof that you're trying.' I guess that explained how she slept peacefully at night.

What I now find strange is for someone who was apparently fully booked and had stressed the painful efforts made to accommodate me in her schedule, how empty the waiting room always was. Once, as my mother was inside, I sat counting the number of calories I had consumed that day having been introduced to the concept by my aunt—an apparent fitness freak who till date will cite various detox diets at the table and religiously follows not a single one. A man in a leather jacket sitting next to me smiled at me when waiting his turn, whilst my mother had her share of enlightenment by the Alzheimer's specialist. With a grandmother at home who was an avid watcher of TV serials, I worryingly instantly recognised him as an actor on one of her daily soaps. Finally, I had a reason to see Nita. Two minutes later, my mother came out and it was time to bid goodbye to my newly made friend who surprisingly waved back—he was probably touched he'd found one of his two fans. Now there's just my grandmother left.

Cut to 2015. I am watching my favourite reality show where a group of fifteen socially frustrated individuals consistently exercise their ability to torture one another, only to make up the next day with a barrage of hugs. I've honestly never felt closer to home. So, sitting in my living room in London, I wait eagerly to see who the new wild card entrant will be. Suddenly, a shady looking (literally wearing orange sunglasses) man walks into the house whose identity is only revealed by the promo for what was 'tomorrow's episode'. The man was none other than my long lost friend—the actor in the waiting room who received the same mental guidance as me. My immediate reflex was to reach out for my phone and furiously vote for him as only I could understand why he was the way he was. Over the next couple of days of his short stay on the show, he woke up at four o'clock in the morning to sing a hymn, hit on the host, and locked a woman in the bathroom.

However, don't make the mistake of taking this as a sign of mediocrity on Nita's part as a shrink. For driving her patients insane so that they did indeed have a reason to come back to her was a genius tactic on her part, and one that contributed to her success.

Her nonchalance about it can be best explained by another of her desk quotes—*'Expect the worst and you will never be disappointed.'*

Chapter 2

Coco

The underdog of today usually becomes the hero of tomorrow, but often such tales contain both joy and sorrow.

A family tradition that has remained constant for aeons is that of keeping dogs. From the guard dog to the dachshund flown in from Hyderabad for my fifth birthday to my brother . . . our house has always been full of dogs. Coco, who was a family favourite, certainly deserves to be given the place he forcibly etched into my heart.

I was downstairs in the kitchen when I suddenly dropped a pair of scissors. Reaching underneath the table, I suddenly peered into two sea green eyes in the darkness that were embedded in a polished, jet black coat that appeared to be velvet from a distance. I brought my face closer because you can really never be sure what animal you're seeing: a rat, a raccoon, a snake, a lizard, or a baby bear. Suddenly, before I could decipher whose eyes I was peering into, or giving me a chance to exert a reflex, it lifted its two-centimetre long nails and dragged them through my right cheek.

I started bleeding profusely as the wound was unusually deep, and a doctor was called home immediately. The culprit was of course one of the dogs—the black dachshund—Coco. I barely had any interaction with Coco apart from witnessing him engage in a war the other day with Pepsi—a white Pomeranian whose organs were slowly shutting down. Every year, my aunt would drag Pepsi back from his grave by inserting some kind of life into him even if that involved taking out his faulty body parts one after the other. I was very familiar with Coco's propensity for violence regardless of the fact that this knowledge was useless given his ability to camouflage with anything black.

After that episode, my mother has always claimed Coco to be her 'soul dog' which really leaves nothing to be said. Nonetheless, that one split second has left me scarred for life as I carry till date a deep scar, visible from a decent distance on my right cheek. It's even marked in most legal documents as my 'distinguishing feature'. No matter how many ointments, creams, and lotions I've used, they've all had minimal effect in the long term. Now, I view it as my battle wound in a war I lost to nature, and a lesson for the future—never to stick my face in a dog's, no matter how tempted I am.

I strictly maintained a distance from Coco for the next year, which was a more difficult task than one could imagine. There were times when he approached me sitting on the stairs, sticking his face into mine and looking into my eyes and I had no choice but to walk away. During that period, I watched him religiously eat chicken and Hershey's kisses to give him the energy needed for his feuds with Pepsi. Once, whilst walking past, I witnessed a wispy ball of cotton wool shedding as it rolled down the stairs as Coco watched triumphant from the top with his leg sticking out having just kicked his nemesis.

Two nights later, as Coco sat in a corner eating his barbecue chicken leg, he felt more famished than usual given his participation in what seemed like a two-hour banquet. He must have consumed thirteen chicken legs by the end of the evening and understandably headed upstairs to my grandparents' room to take a break. I had no choice but to follow him, given that Pepsi was also rolled on the carpet in the corner. However, Coco was entirely uninterested in moving a paw. With the television blaring in the background, he rolled on his back and stared longingly at the screen. He closed his eyes wafting into a deep sleep as I saw his stomach move inches up and down as he took heavy breaths. I positioned myself on the lazy boy and continued watching the movie. Thirty minutes later, I heard a croak and turned around to see Coco's arms and legs in the air, his eyes popping out as he was choking on a chicken bone. I immediately rang the bell for somebody to come up and help. But it was too late. Coco had passed away. He ate, and he ate, and he ate—at least he died doing what he loved.

This sudden shock to our family was difficult to digest much like the chicken. Coco was entitled to a decent burial like with all our other dogs. So my mother, Aunty Jasmine, and I took him in the car and drove to the nearest graveyard. We had to find a tombstone for his body quickly at eleven o'clock at night in an empty cemetery. Finally, we caught sight of a figure moving in the dark—what emerged to be the watchman. Explaining our situation and giving him a generous tip won us both sympathy and prayers as he scoured for an empty space in the cemetery. He left us hanging in the rain with Coco's body for ten minutes. Finally, he emerged to reveal bad news. To be fair, it was in sync with how the rest of the evening had been. 'But there is one option,' he trailed off staring at the grave in front of us. So, together, the four of us dug into the soil in the dark until we found a base for Coco. We placed his body lovingly there as we bid him a tearful goodbye. Today, Coco unknowingly shares his grave with Father Joseph.

This episode asserted two facts to me. Firstly, my distrust of birds is justified. *Secondly, we should stop thinking about whom we spend this lifetime with—it's the afterlife we should worry about. But if dog is man's best friend then I'm sure Father Joseph has no problem.*

Chapter 3

Floods

When thrown into the deep end, you can either sink or swim. But what happens if the second option is not even an 'option'?

The floods of 2006 were a milestone event for most Indians who were in Mumbai at the time. It not only polished our DIY (do-it-yourself) skills, but also tested the limits of our creativity and ability to stay tightly knit against all odds. At times of an unexpected crisis, how well you stick together is greatly dependent on how well you individually channel your creative energies to find solutions. One man simply can't lead a family as diverse as ours—somebody else thinking for you is never a good option. Nobody expected the heavy shower—a daily happening during the monsoon season—to eventually seep into our house by flowing through the back door.

I was alone at home on the second floor as my entire family were out—my mother had taken Sid to the dentist; my grandmother had gone to play cards; my grandfather, Uncle Keith and Aunty Jasmine were at work. Zara wasn't born yet. I was on my way downstairs from the bedroom making my way towards the dining table on the ground floor when suddenly, Singh, our chef, started alerting all the boys. The heavy rain outside was flowing through the back door of the kitchen despite it being locked. Soon, the refrigerator was floating and so were the staff. My instant reflex was to be selfless and save myself because they would need me later. Whilst on my great escape on my way upstairs, I passed the sympathy evoking watchman and our German shepherd who simply could not be outside in this weather. Luckily, I happened to be one of the few in the household who Lucky did not bark, at and so I escorted him upstairs to my grandparents' bedroom as we moved up a floor to escape the growing water level on the ground floor. This was a game we continued to play until there were no floors left, and the only option was to rebuild the bungalow. Given our present predicament, it was an option we would need to revisit in the future.

Of course, none of the other family members were even aware of this situation with phone lines down across the city; finally, the cordless outside came to life after having received a thorough thrashing as I made quick calls informing everyone urging them to return in time given the weather before it was too late . . . for me. Suddenly, in the middle of an animated, impassioned plea to my aunt to come home as soon as possible, I turned to find the cupboard door torn down, lying on the floor. Tying Lucky to the handle, the only option available was obviously not creative thinking.

So, now with this 50-kilo German shepherd lying on the bed, who could not be let out as he threatened the lives of all. Outside the room, I heard a kerfuffle in the corridor.

As expected, Singh and his team had joined in the floor up game and were now holding forte in the barroom upstairs, having left the kitchen. By this time, the entire ground floor was submerged.

It really was difficult to tell when day transcended into night given the power cuts and lights out at 2 p.m. itself. Luckily, my grandparents, Sid, and my mother made it back in one piece. Thankfully, Aunty Jasmine arrived five hours later. The good news was that she arrived not in one piece but two. Despite her harsh features and baritone voice, she was soft at heart, as Catherine in her grave can vouch for. This need to help others included being the weekend babysitter for mothers wishing to visit the sunbed, and walking her neighbour's dogs even if she was fed up with her own. As the downpour continued, Aunty Jasmine had invited a lady she met outside the office whose fiancé had been unable to make the journey to pick her up. My aunt offered her a lift home despite knowing that our driver himself had not learnt to power a car through water yet. So they hopped onto a stranger's bike for what was probably the most dangerous and thrilling ride of their lives, as they dodged vipers and sewer rats swimming in what was essentially a sea.

That evening, we faced our first crisis, which Aunty Jasmine did not help with at all—dinner. Anand, an incredibly efficient staff member, had somehow managed to sweep water out of the kitchen with a broom; how, we really don't know. Obviously, there was no option of cooking a fresh meal—frozen foods were the only undamaged items due to the altitude of their position. In a house totally pitch dark, someone had to make their way downstairs and prepare the meal. Singh admirably stepped up to the challenge, proving his loyalty to the family, yet again. Peering from the barroom—our communal hideout—we watched him tread down the soaking stairs in trepidation as he soon disappeared into an abyss of darkness, perhaps never to be seen again. That evening, Singh risked being electrocuted whilst frying six bags of frozen samosas in the darkness. Obviously, what would otherwise be a ten-minute task understandably took much longer given the wild, life-threatening circumstances in which Singh was cooking. One-and-a-half hour later, he emerged up the stairs with sixty-five samosas on a tray—the only undamaged food left in the kitchen. I don't know how many samosas I ate that night, but I remember thinking it would be my last meal; this resulted in fever the next morning, and a lifelong vow to never touch a samosa again.

The next day, we realised living in the bungalow was just not feasible with the floods, so we had to move. 'How would we do that?' asked Aunty Jasmine. As usual, she had no idea. So my four-year-old brother was carried in a bucket on top of my uncle's head, as I was hurled on someone else's shoulders during a gruesome walk to my aunt's penthouse down the road. When people have the audacity to turn around and tell me how I've never struggled, obviously oblivious to the number of social sacrifices I have made in order to dedicate myself wholly to academics (which somehow doesn't count unless it is something materialistic), I narrate this tale of wading through the cholera infested water from our bungalow to our penthouse in Juhu. Having reached the building, we were safe and sound . . . if the water could transcend twenty-six floors, then the only higher floor was heaven, to which I'm never going to be allowed in anyway. After roughly ten days when the rains had subsided, we decided it was safe to return to the bungalow.

Somehow, the bungalow has never been the same since. We were lucky in the sense that no mass deconstruction or colossal damage was done, but time and again, we receive small yet significant reminders of the past that bring us further to earth. My grandfather's sauna room on the terrace seems to be his favourite hangout on a Sunday afternoon. So two years ago, when he was beautifying himself for three hours inside the room, a telling incident occurred that scarred many. As the drivers sat downstairs relaxing in the parking lot, one dozing off on a wooden chair, the other drinking his daily tea, suddenly, they felt a piece of cement crumble down on their heads. As they looked up into a cloud of dust and steam, they saw my grandfather turn only to discover the external wall of the sauna had fallen having been the only room that wasn't refurbished after the floods. But the cracks in the house are the chinks in our armour—the lines on our forehead, which are unlikely to be removed via Botox. Such an incident still hasn't prevented my grandfather from pursuing his weekly routine, for traditions are best carried out in a new environment.

The bungalow is still being rebuilt, so as one can see, we've never stopped trying.

Chapter 4

Sandra

'Give me a child till he's seven and I'll give you a man,'
said Aristotle once upon a time. If the company you keep is
instrumental to your development, then that explains a lot
about why we turned out the way we did.

When I was younger, my first babysitter—Sandra—who
looked after me from the time I was four until ten in
London, was quite the enigma. We still haven't been able to
figure out what we exactly paid her to do in those six years,
given her distorted opinion of what her job entailed, until
she was replaced by Delna in 2009, who shocked us with
her work ethic and lack of demands. Sandra was wrecking
havoc in the house until then, with her theft and bunking
off work.

The strangest part about all of this was that she didn't even
make an effort to hide what she was doing. We appreciate
that it was all in the open. Why we didn't fire her for six
years is an answer only my mother has, although it probably
involves explaining how she never had the heart to tell her to
leave. As a result, we waited for her to personally express her
desire to return to her home in Sri Lanka. Sandra was also

a pathological liar. Once, for her fiftieth birthday, she took my mother to Peter Jones so that she can buy her a watch, having lost her own. Agreeing to do so, my mother readily gave a gold Longines model to her as a gift. Two days later, when Sandra's older watch miraculously turned up on her wrist, she claimed she had found it in the garbage. What she forgot to mention was that she herself must have placed it in the bin bag.

What makes Sandra still unfathomable was her gift-wrapped package of lies she presented us with every year. This often involved changing her nationality, family details, and religion, to make her seem in better favour with us. Assuming us to be Muslim upon her appointment, she claimed to follow the same religion. When finding out two years later that we did not practise Islam given that two Ramadan seasons had passed without anybody in the house fasting, she explained that she had lied and was actually Hindu. We accepted her decision as readily as she had when she presented herself to us as Muslim, given that acceptance of all religions is a norm in our family. We celebrate Christian, Muslim, and Hindu festivals, and pray to only one god—the one that does not belong to any particular faith but all. When my mother revealed she went to church every Tuesday to a friend, she was asked whether she was a Christian. Tomorrow, if I find the most peace in Buddhist teachings, I'll adopt that too. No faith is higher than another and as long as you're not fanatical—you have the freedom to imbibe, combine, and intertwine whatever faiths and beliefs you wish to that give you the most peace of mind, including atheism. For us, religion has been more about having a higher force to look up to and pray to for hope and guidance. So Sandra's constant desire to change her religion every few years out of god knows what fear of us, was continually baffling. It also didn't exactly help that she continually referred to my grandmother as 'grandma' despite being a couple of years older.

Sandra had always told us she was from Sri Lanka, which nobody had any problems with. She also claimed that her parents and sister had died leaving behind her niece and nephew whom she treated like her own children. This would explain her intensely loud and emotional daily phone conversations with them using the home landline, never minding that it prevented us from calling our grandparents. Often there were tears, barking, and even growling, as Sandra had ferociously expressive verbal interactions with Marissa and Johnny. When Marissa moved to London, Sandra suggested that she could teach me knitting every Saturday morning (these were the days of no Spanish). Being paid a handsome sum of 100 pounds for one and half hours, Marissa would visit me every weekend when my mother had set out to collect my brother from football practice, leaving Sandra, Marissa, and I alone at home. Often during the session in my bedroom, Sandra would step inside to argue with Marissa in Sri Lankan. Obviously discussing an intimate family matter, I would leave the room to give them the required privacy. That was the structure most of our lessons followed until I finally revealed what was happening behind closed doors to my mother and they were politely put to a halt.

Sandra's other antics frequently cost us dearly. She would often announce before leaving for the day that she'd taken with her a few bags of rice and boxes of Chinese tea because she was having guests over for dinner. The amazing ability she had to make us feel like trespassers in our own home was strangely incredible. Once, I walked into the bathroom to catch her in the middle of a shower. Peeking from behind the shower curtain, she shouted, 'Can't you see? I'm washing.' Oh dear, I had caught her in the act. I ran outside deleting the visual from my mind so that I could sleep peacefully at night. Another time whilst passing my brother's bedroom, I found Sandra sitting on the bed watching East Enders as she helped herself to a bowl of popcorn. Two minutes later, when walking by the kitchen, the carpet felt damp as I saw water trickling out of the closed door. She had left the tap running for an hour.

When you've had a long run, it's not a bad idea to make your goodbye short. So forgetting she had initially introduced herself as Sri Lankan, Sandra said it was time for her to return to her home in South India. We happily said our farewells and appointed a new housekeeper, Delna, who this time really was from Sri Lanka.

Often those from the smallest places create a stir across the globe. Size doesn't matter.

Chapter 5

Alcoholism

The bottle seems to be an old friend to most of us to forget our worries, create new ones, and rue the day we were born.

Unfortunately or fortunately, I've never seemed to take a liking to drinking—I don't need alcohol to get a rush, I'm high on life. Booze and my family share a special relationship starting from 40 years ago when my grandfather was certified as one of the few owners of a 125 year-old bottle of Chivas Regal in India. Ever since then, our collection has expanded to the humble Old Monk—of which my aunt being a simpleton (read: lacking any taste) is a loyal fan to Black Labels, Gold Labels, and not to mention the floor-to-ceiling wine cabinet which we view as the poor man's whisky.

My grandparents used to be greatly fond of entertaining; but after a knee surgery, one eye operation, and two strokes, they are slightly less able to dance the night away to a live band and handle a sharp hangover. Nevertheless, when the time comes to do so, they step up to the challenge and complete the task with grace, which often involves my grandmother excusing herself halfway with her standard dialogue—'I can't see anything at night.' This would evoke sympathy from all of us—if only my mother hadn't caught her five years ago happily watching another one of her daily soaps that blared on the TV in her bedroom.

It appears that there was someone else in the house strangely similar to my grandmother—an unlikely candidate; Nagamma, the newly imported cleaner from our house in Mangalore. Words cannot do her appearance justice, but if Yoda had a female counterpart complete with the wispy hairs and green alien like complexion, Nagamma fit this description. But bear in mind, 'Nags' was deceptively old; her age really was just a number for her and a secret to us. Much like my grandmother, she too, spent most of her days watching the same daily soap in secret. The only difference was, whilst my grandmother watched from a leather lazy boy as our ageing dachshund lay on her lap drooling on her silk dressing gown, Nagamma made her own corner in the larder where she craftily sat concealed by a pile of tender coconuts. This secret place was such a well-kept one that soon, the entire barrage of staff joined in this clandestine act by watching behind her as she cackled periodically, helping herself to a pile of snacks including Charbonnel et Walker marc de champagne truffles bought from Harrods that had been given to her to place in my grandmother's fridge. She was a shady character to say the least—there were even conspiracy theories that she had pushed her husband from a tree when they were picking apples.

With an incredibly hardworking staff who were treated with the utmost care and respect, no one ever even thought of pointing a finger at a cook or cleaner when a piece of jewellery was lost (such as my grandmother's heart-shaped diamond ring in 2007), or whenever a mishap occurred. The possibility of theft or one of our own usurping resources was never even present in our minds—instead, blaming ourselves for negligence resulting in loss of possessions, was the only option. Over a period of six months, my grandfather started noticing a strange taste in his beloved nightly drink—Glenfiddich single malt 18 years—hadn't ever tasted this bland leading him to double his number of drinks, until the sensation kicked in. Nonetheless, something was fishy, and there's only so long for which playing the blame game was fun. Nobody quite had any explanation for this phenomenon—was the alcohol too old? Not possible, given it was bought at Heathrow a year ago. Had my grandmother poisoned it? Maybe, but I'm sure we would have seen results earlier. For many nights we all slept perplexed, when one day my grandmother— needing to increase her sugar level—opened the barroom door at three o'clock in the morning, only to find Nags walking a few steps in front of her to the cabinet. Acting as if nothing else needed to be said, my grandmother walked out of the room ready to recount the tale to us the next morning.

It was easy to infer what had been happening. Every night since she had arrived, Nagamma had been going into the barroom—her local watering hole, and drowning her troubles in my grandfather's whisky. What she did cleverly after that was promptly fill it to the top with water, which explained both its diluted taste and why the whisky never seemed to be running out. You have to hand it to her;

she had exquisite taste and the tact of a Machiavellian. Suddenly, my grandmother believed the toilet cleaner placed in her bathroom cupboard by Nags was actually a weapon she would use on her one of these nights. As a result, not only was an additional person added to the list to fear at night but one room was locked everyday at eleven at night—the barroom.

In case people wonder how we could have made such a great inference from Nagamma's sole presence that night at the barroom, let me assure you there is another conspiracy theory. It's really a toss-up between the two. It could have very well been my grandmother who sneaked into the barroom at night and drank to her heart's content, only to fill the bottle till the top and blame all on the shadiest member of the kitchen team. If so, the great gambler definitely could see at night.

Despite this heavy drinking and predilection for violence, Nagamma has still managed to outlive Catherine—she will probably outlive all of us for which she must be congratulated.

The matriarch in every house may not be kind and wise, but she is always high and mighty.

Chapter 6

Phuket

Many places you visit will make you wonder what is wrong with the people. But only few will make you wonder what is wrong with yourself.

I stared at the glass cabinet of precious stones in front of me. It had been an eventful trip to Thailand so far—I had nearly fallen off during an elephant ride through the jungle and a number of meanings had been lost in translation. Little did I know that the most happening and wild night was yet to come—a family dinner. My grandmother asked my mother, Aunty Jasmine, and myself to select earrings of our choice made from our individual birthstones—never mind that mine was peridot, which I felt had nothing to do with my ferocious Leo-like personality. But for the old lady, astrology trumps logic everyday; and I believe perception overrides reality, so I gave in.

Having bought our jewellery, we awaited the arrival of Uncle Keith and my grandfather who had gone for an authentic Thai massage at the St Regis—our hotel of choice. They looked and smelt visibly changed as if having bathed in all the stock of Jo Malone and come back. It was dinnertime and my grandfather's persistence to eat 'authentic Thai food' had gotten to the point of being a relentless drone in the background. Having asked our hotel for a recommendation, we set off in an SUV large enough to incorporate seven wholesome and ever-expanding bodies. The one word to describe that car journey would be 'pungent'. Having apparently rolled in sandalwood, jasmine leaves, and raw vanilla pods, the men in the car appeared to be in desperate need of testosterone patches. Along the way, we passed the only place in the world that could make Mumbai appear as a hamlet—a flea market in South East Asia. Fake handbags, candy coloured plastic goods, and Barbie pink mobile phones were the most popular items on sale. On my right, I turned to see a small boutique-like store with the sign, having been literally translated from English, 'Hand job—Nails and Spa'. At least, my grandfather and Uncle Keith didn't get their massages there. During this ride, my grandfather frequently sneezed inhaling his own fragrance. I had to agree with the world—he was a powerful man in every way, namely his ability to stir the senses—both our own and his.

The driver pulled up to a foliage decorated entrance and said, 'Enjoy.'

'Okay. Come in one hour,' my grandfather said.

'Are you sure?' the driver enquired worriedly. It was almost as if he had foreseen what a unique experience we were about to have, and so wished to prolong the duration.

'Now time for authentic Thai,' my grandfather said like the broken record he enjoyed being. This highly recommended authentic Thai food serving restaurant was so wonderfully quaint and homegrown that the locals seemed to have decided to give the management team (consisting of the family itself) privacy by not visiting them at all. We were the sole diners in this outdoor restaurant as a flute player—most likely one of the prodigal sons who graced us with a rendition of what I'm sure was some folk song—moaned in the corner. After having paused to take a break to talk on the phone, his volume exceeded that of all eight of ours.

'Now to eat authentic Thai,' my grandfather announced for the fifth time now desperately trying to draw out some kind of reaction, namely enthusiasm, given our universal silence so far. This was to mask what we knew would not go down well with a group of unadventurous eaters only comfortable with the big three meats—chicken, pork, and lamb—which seemed too mainstream in South East Asia to be included on any of the menus instead favouring shark fin soup and every kind of fish in the tropical aquarium we had at home.

A woman appeared who had an interesting hairstyle that combined rock and electric shock as she said in her thick accent—'The manager will be with you shortly.' Lo and behold, our manager is the same man whose memorable performance we were previously subjected to on the flute.

So the flute player-cum-manager-cum-waiter (cum I'm sure cleaner and cook) asked, 'What is the order?'

'We want authentic Thai.' Of course, the obvious answer. 'Two vegetarians,' he gestured at my uncle and I. A look of disgust overcame our waiter's face as if a crime had been committed—I couldn't tell whether it was our dietary choice, or if he had gotten a whiff of my grandfather's bodily scent post massage.

'What else?' he asked this time truly hoping we'd order something for he may have just killed himself if he had to cook with purely bean curd and vegetables.

'Chicken, anything with chicken,' my grandparents cried out in unison.

'Some fries as well,' asserted my aunt. 'One tom yum soup too,' she called after him.

When he left towards the kitchen, my grandmother called out, 'He better walk quicker if he's going to cook our food as well.' We all laughed at the situation we were in, giving into my grandfather's bid to eat authentic Thai would not only send us to our early graves but also drive home the point of why being too authentic is never a great idea.

Forty-five minutes later, we sat batting mosquitoes, more fearing a prolonged stay in Phuket than malaria, and still no food had arrived. My grandfather summoned our manager friend asking, 'Where's our food?' making no bones about hiding his annoyance.

'He's just preparing it,' he said shaken up by the fact somebody could actually emote in his restaurant. I don't know who he was referring to when he said 'he'. He didn't need to pretend there was an expansive staff—it was quite clear he'd sent them all home with his flute playing. Only he was left to prepare our dinner—we both had no choice.

He came back to us with our much-desired fare and unceremoniously placed down a plate of undercooked chicken and some fried prawns. What was most bafflingly brazen was the lump of uncooked bean curd thrown onto a plate and a pile of leafy greens, which appeared to have been plucked from the foliage surrounding us. Clearly, he had no respect for vegetarians.

'What is this?' my grandfather asked pointing at the prawns.

'Fries,' he answered coolly in a tone that made him seem on autopilot.

'Do you know what fries are? French fries,' my grandfather groaned, hitting breaking point. Manager stared blankly. 'Potato fries, fry potatoes in oil and give them to us.' Silent for a few minutes, this was the first time he looked like he was genuinely trying to figure out what my grandfather was trying to tell him.

'I have one potato.'

At this point, my grandfather raised up his hands gesturing for him to be gone as he barked 'aaaarh'. We are the only family on earth who would order french fries in an authentic Thai restaurant.

It is not the entrance everyone remembers as much as the exit. So here was our manager's final chance to clean out this mess. 'Fingerbowls,' my grandfather ordered once we had finished without even starting our meal. There was no 'yes' or 'no', just a silent departure on the manager's part as he set out to possibly retrieve a club from the kitchen to knock us out. Didn't he know his flute playing was sufficient enough? He emerged soon, although with no visible weapon in hand; he placed a couple of cooking vessels on our table filled with water in which my family washed their hands. These were our delicate fingerbowls.

After this cleansed, it was time to bid goodbye to this one-man crew. Sympathising with his situation, my grandfather still gave him a hefty tip, as custom doesn't vary if the customer is the same. Before leaving, we surprisingly thanked the manager for dinner; we both had suffered this evening, but at least, we emerged with a good story out of what was daily torture for him.

Next was a trip to the Hand Job salon.

Chapter 7

Nita 2.0

Love is apparently blind, it also favours Yin and Yang more than peas in a pod.

Going to our country house in Mangalore was a trip dreaded by our family. The Grecian style architecture with a colonnaded frontier made of marble, lush lawns and never ending gardens sound like a dream, but we always had one question as a family: 'Why in Mangalore?' Going back to our roots was never a joyride for the younger generation of the family, by which I mean everyone apart from my grandparents—days entailing no Wi-Fi, poor mobile network, the fear of what animals would emerge behind you whilst in the shower . . . you really were in harmony with nature. A number of esteemed individuals—film directors, politicians, and foreign friends—have all chosen this as their residence of choice for summer holidays and we're constantly told how beautiful our home is. We don't realise how lucky we are and we probably never will. For some reason, nobody in my family is apologetic about that. Mangalore only ever seemed exciting to us when an unlikely revelation was made to us in another continent.

A while back, we decided to take a two-week holiday in Rome; the lucky members of this family excursion were my brother Sid, my mother, Aunty Jasmine, Zara, and I. Having been warned about relentless mugging and all sorts of other crimes that take place in broad daylight, we were disappointed to find that nothing of the sort happened with us. The closest we got to being rough, down, and dirty, was drinking from the fountain opposite the Spanish Steps and Prada flagship store. Nonetheless, back in the hotel room we were in for a surprise that hit all of us like a thunderbolt. Over room service (eating is our favourite pastime), my aunt asked my eleven-year-old brother, 'So Sid, have you ever liked any girls?'

My brother and I went to exclusive all-boys/all-girls private schools in London. That had nothing to do with us not being trustworthy or likely to be distracted—if you see us in person, you'll know why. There simply weren't any options to choose from as all the men and women in the world seemed to have had a private conference to exclude us from being considered desirable. It is often said that desperate times call for desperate measures, and I suppose that is the only way to digest the piece of news we were about to hear.

'Well, there is one girl.' He answered sheepishly and then turned away like a blushing bride. After relentless teasing and torturing on every single person in the room's part (all female), he finally gave in. Now, my brother has been mainly surrounded by women his entire life. As a result, he has developed rather effeminate mannerisms himself, or what we view as conventionally girly—he cries at the drop of a hat, takes great offense to comments about his non-existent love life, and often buries his weeklong woes by climbing in bed with a bucket of Ben and Jerry's to watch a chick flick. So, in the midst of his huffing and puffing, he finally let out the name of his beloved—Nita. No, this isn't the psychiatrist—if you can really call her that—for I don't believe as powerful as a degree maybe that it entirely translates into reality. Nita was also the name of one of the staff, Gopi's daughter, in our house in Mangalore.

I want to clarify that house help in our family are treated as a part of it. In fact, no matter how many chickens are burnt, how many times a driver loses his way going to the same place, or how many holidays they wish to take ('Today is my cousin's brother in law's dog's vet's wedding Madam'), never once have I heard any member of my family chide or even rebuke them in anyway. 'Criticism can be constructive and destructive' is a strong belief in my household, and only the former is worth it and can be achieved with politeness and respect. Neither have we ever resorted to the, 'What will people say?' logic which seems to have shattered the majority of dreams worldwide. Class is something I don't see as a barrier between two potential mates. But, nothing could have prepared us for my brother who had previously never even called a girl 'pretty' or expressed any interest in the opposite sex, to be nursing a silent crush on Nita, Gopi's daughter.

The obvious question—which everyone was thinking and only my aunt could articulate—'Why?' had an interesting response. I wondered what could have made the simple, oiled braid sporting Nita, attractive to my brother. It's not like he had great taste to start with and looks are by no means the only measure of desirability, but they didn't even speak the same language.

His answer was touchingly simple and sickening at the same time. 'Because I like the way she looks after Zara and takes care of her.' Suddenly, we were all silently transported down memory lane to watch a movie that made more sense than it did whilst it was in action. A young Sid blowing water balloons as Nita handed him more from the bucket. A slightly older British boy, trying to show off his newly developed, fake accent, whilst teaching Zara the alphabet as a shy Nita peered from behind the pillar. And now, an eleven- year- old Sid eating butter chicken as he slyly stares into the kitchen, trying to decipher the face behind the veil as she stuck by Gopi's side helping him to prepare dinner.

Today, after having received a sufficient amount of bullying from the family, he barely takes Nita's name. But I have to say that whenever she offers him a glass of water and he mouths with his voluptuous lips, 'Thank you', their chemistry is electrifying, to say the least.

Ever since then, Mangalore has been the hub of quite a few unlikely romances. As a gift to Zara, my grandmother bought her two rabbits—a beige one, and a white one. My cousin was given the liberty to name them, which was not a great idea given her newfound exposure to American and British TV shows. Rosie Buttons, she pronounced the white one; and Salman Khan—the only Indian actor she was familiar with. Over the next few days of Rosie and Salman's arrival, I came across them in various compromising positions across the garden. Unsurprisingly, one of them— Salman, was found lying exhausted two days later with what was suspected to be an illness. Zara and Aunty Jasmine took on the responsibility of bringing him to the local vet—not so local if you take into account the two-hour car journey. We were pleased to see all three in high spirits, -although Salman had just been given a painkiller, which would explain his bloodshot eyes and delirium. Zara shouted, "'Salman is fine. He's also a girl.' It appears that both animals and humans are rather open-minded in Mangalore about love—probably because the options available in a concrete jungle are clearly missing.

Often the most rural places have the maximum number of skeletons in the closet. It's more difficult to find them.

Chapter 8

The Plant

There's nothing more empowering than a fast metabolic rate.

I can't quite tell whether my family is fat or thin. My grandparents, having had to deal with various health issues such as diabetes, high and low blood pressure, and glaucoma, have been forced to rather than wholeheartedly participate in yoga and underwater aerobics. My mother makes an effort to fit into her designer wear, my aunt tries, and my brother and I don't really bother. But we wear the clothes we want, most of us are fortunately in good health and can be active for a long duration without fainting or perspiring unnecessarily.

I was 11 when I was first called fat, and it affected me in the sense of changing my perception on what I viewed as thin or not. My grandfather's sister who is only allowed home when my grandmother is in a good mood (once every six months), sat on the sofa and pointed at me saying—'My grandson is ten per cent overweight much like her.' I wanted to pack her off home without dinner. This didn't underwhelm me or hurt me because one look at her was enough to prove she lacked a reality check.

The perception we build of ourselves in my family may be self-deprecatory, but it's still always in sync with reality. The idea of having a bloated image of how good looking we are or how thin we are is simply not an option. That's not because we don't give these facets importance—we certainly do—but we just accepted a long time back that how we look is not in our control, and there's no point messing with the features you were naturally given as they somehow go together even if they're mismatched.

Additionally, having spent ample time with a friend's mother who is a plastic surgeon and having heard the horrors from the horse's mouth, I have been put off for another lifetime (I'm already in my sixth according to an astrologer my mother saw in a candlelit den). I can also spot the signs of various surgeries from a distance. If you've noticed someone's jaw line widening over time as their face appears to be broadening, it's only the skin previously pinned by a Botox job sagging. No thanks. Having a reality check is the only check you need because that is your passport to being fearless, and no matter how many film actors and esteemed professionals praise my grandmother's physical beauty, her unaffected nature has taught us that.

Nonetheless, we've all tried to follow a diet at some point that most likely backfired. I remember reading an article on how sprouts was Courtney Cox's favourite go-to food item when she needed to be in particularly trim shape since the time of 'Friends'. Sprouts are not a food item we keep at home for its lack of widespread appeal to the family. Luckily, the day of reading the article we happened to be heading to JW Marriott for brunch—a family tradition.

Whilst scouring the buffet, I internally cried whilst watching a chef place a pizza in a wood fire oven and finally spotted some green nonsense from afar. The sprouts were arranged artfully in glass cups and placed on a stand atop the green marble salad table. I took two of the cups, as this was all I would eat for lunch. Thinking it was a bit much and conscious of my allergies (only to nuts so far, but hopefully to vegetables soon), I put one back and replaced it with a piece of lettuce. What a nourishing meal—I couldn't wait to fill my stomach with a garden. Sitting down at the table, I realised there was simply no way I could eat plain sprouts and so I ground a heavy shower of salt and pepper to knock some taste into it. Praying to the one god I know representing those of every religion, cursing the voluptuous woman sitting near me eating cheesecake, and looking forward to finally wearing the white jeans I had bought, I dug my spoon to the very bottom of the container so that it was filled with greens. At least the chef had the decency to fill the bottom with a layer of black truffle to infuse some kind of flavour.

The green sprouts had a funny, bitter flavour. I had zero expectations, but I was still disappointed. At this point, I noticed one of the waiters shuffling his feet, backing and advancing near me. He must have been in love with me. I was happy for him to join a group called everybody. Once again, I dug a spoonful of sprouts and brought it closer to my mouth until I heard a voice interrupting me—'Ma'am'. Oh god, this really wasn't a time to praise my unique and exotic beauty. I proceeded to finish my spoonful when again, I was cut—'Ma'am, you're eating the plant.' I was disgusted. The sprouts were not actually sprouts but leaves taken from the Marriot's greenhouse and placed in the middle of the salad table for decoration. The black truffle was soil. I also figured I actually had no idea what sprouts even looked like and was a complete and utter idiot. Luckily, the waiter disappeared. He was probably more relieved than I was, having saved the life of someone he was in love with. Embarrassment is an emotion I stopped feeling after relieving myself in the middle of Harrods as a toddler. But really, everything is okay now.

Obviously, my family welcomed the news of my eating a plant with roaring laughter. Ever since they warn me not to consume every tree we pass. Trying out this diet unsuccessfully only reasserted the pointlessness in stepping so far out of your comfort zone that you feel none at all. Today, I have absolutely no idea what my weight is, having not checked for years, but I fit into the clothes I buy for myself and given how lucky I am to be able to afford whatever I want to eat, I think it's almost criminal not to take advantage of the options I am blessed to have. There's nothing wrong in being an herbivore, and there was nothing wrong with the woman eating the cheesecake next to me.

There was something wrong with Courtney Cox.

Chapter 9

The Great Gambler

Late to bed and late to rise, makes a woman sharp, secretive,
and an overall surprise.

Over practising the same skill continually nearly daily over
many years often leads to burnout. However, this has not
been the case with my grandmother whose skilful card
playing over decades has earned her the title of the 'Great
Gambler'. I find it strange that gambling is seen as a vice,
suggesting that most people who enjoy doing so are roadside
thugs or bootleggers wasting their incomes on blackjack
where the stakes are high enough to massage their egos.

But this is very different from the reality myself, along with
many others, have been exposed to. Every other day, a herd
of my grandmother's friends come home to play in a setting
that has earned the unfortunate title of a 'kitty party'. I have
no idea what happens inside, but her barrage of partners in
pleasure make their presence felt. Often, whilst dining at
the table, the white marble would start vibrating, instigating
the fear of an earthquake inside me. This would happen
whenever one of her friends with a posterior the size of a

beach ball would make their way up flights of stairs to the card room, unaware they were making waves as they moved.

Even if this pursuit made my grandmother relatively modern, she still infused an element of tradition in the process. Two hours before her friends were due to arrive she would start beautifying herself. She would ask me to come into the card room during the middle of playing, to say hello to all her friends, including and especially her. My grandmother proved herself to be a superlative actress, for suddenly when I'd walk into the card room, she would feign an expression of surprise as she'd exclaim, 'What are you doing here?' This would be followed by innocent laughter whilst her crafty eyes looked at me gesturing for me to step forward and give her a hug. When I did exactly that—my grandmother would add more nuances to her performance by turning to her friends in the middle of a staged embrace, exclaiming, 'My grandchildren love spending time with me. I tell them to do their own thing but they insist on being with me!' This may sound derisive towards us, but she meant it in the most loving way possible, and endearingly convinced herself as she said so.

Earlier on as a six-year-old, my grandmother would give me exclusive access to her card room when action was on. Whoever was out of the game first was punished by having to teach and play black jack with me for the rest of the session. Of course, I didn't last the entire time; my main motivation for playing was the afternoon tea served at three o'clock. Over time, I watched her friends consume every possible vegetable that had been deep fried in oil enough to give a cholesterol attack to the yeti. After this two-hour-long meal, they would play till heartburn set in and then return home to eat dinner.

Sometimes, men would be allowed into the 'kitty party', not changing the dynamics at all but further feminising the group. Dara, my grandmother's jeweller, would occasionally join in only to shower her with gifts every two weeks. Initially, we were excited at the prospect of receiving, compared to all the giving we participated in, and bubbles rose out of our heads with rubies and precious gems enclosed in pearl encrusted cases. This wasn't quite what Dara had given my grandmother, but we opened the box to find a beautifully decorated Christmas cake nonetheless. Two minutes later, I had an allergy and Dara was blacklisted.

Thanks to my grandmother's hobby, there was a period where our holidays were happening too frequently in the region of South East Asia, given the number of casinos there. We were told that Genting Islands was much like Sun City in South Africa—a holiday we had thoroughly enjoyed the previous year. Instead, we walked into a gimmicky hotel with an indoor rollercoaster and a tattoo parlour. So whilst we ran from pillar to post trying to entertain ourselves with restaurants similar to the one visited in Phuket, and thus finding the appropriate doctors to do the required damage control, the great gambler had a blast from spending her mornings queuing outside the casino to entering before the cleaners at twelve o'clock in the afternoon and eventually calling it an exhilarating night at 10 p.m.

'Let her enjoy her life, god knows how long it will be' is an adage we have been living by for the past decade. Every day, she continually reminds us of her mortality and how she's rarely spent her time doing anything useful. But I strongly disagree. My grandmother always says how she wishes to die in her sleep, as she believes that to be the most peaceful way of passing away.

If, as I believe, the most peaceful way of passing away is to die doing what you love and given the number of hours the great gambler spends at the club, she's guaranteed a blessed afterlife.

Chapter 10

Raoul

The best place to hide oneself is in the most obvious place.

When a visitor comes home who I am not fully acquainted with, my instant response is to hide behind a pillar as they make conversation with another member of my family. In this particular instance, Aunty Jasmine, Uncle Keith, and Zara had come to visit us in London. It so happened that a school friend of Zara's happened to also be staying in Central London, and so both parties decided to take a joint trip to Whipsnade Safari Park, collectively grossing a three-hour journey.

Unfortunately, the meeting point for this excursion was our house, making it difficult for me to repeat history and hide behind the door of the drawing room the last time when our neighbour dropped by unexpectedly. Raoul, Zara's classmate, was going to be accompanied by his parents who Aunty Jasmine described as 'the old variety' expressing how little she was looking forward to being confined in the small space of a van with them for such a long duration. My mother advised me to leave the house five minutes before they arrived, as there was no possible way I could conceal myself given Zara's propensity for taking anybody who came home for a tour.

The concept of time is alien to most Indians, and therefore planning around their exact arrival time was going to be a mammoth task. Of course, our doorbell had to ring when I was in the middle of watching my favourite TV show. How dare I expect to have an uninterrupted spell of watching TV? I beat a hasty dash to my bedroom, only to trip on the rug in the corridor. The doors to our bedrooms are always left open at home for some reason. So forgetting to shun tradition as I normally do, I climbed into my bed and smothered the Siberian goose feather duvet over my face. This was fine as Raoul's family were only going to drop by for five minutes, and their purpose was solely to collect Aunty Jasmine, Uncle Keith, and Zara. They probably were only going to stand outside the door. Why would they want to make long, polite conversation with my mother when they had a long day ahead of them? Nonetheless, there should have been no visible bulge under my blanket in case Zara were to walk in with Raoul. And so I sucked in my stomach so that my washboard abs would be in sync with the lining of the blanket.

Having laid there for more than five minutes (precisely seven), I wondered what exactly was going on. Until I heard the dreaded footsteps of my mother most likely carrying a tray bearing ginger tea and other edibles to convey season's greetings. Oh no, why were snacks being taken in, somebody tell her to take back the beverages! To clarify, it is a tradition in our family not to send any guest home without giving them a meal. I am a wholehearted participant in this and will always pledge my support to similar causes any one of us wishes to flag up. But at this point, I was most worried about my mortality. Only to figure out fifteen minutes into being under there that the heating was also on—this made me feel as if I was in a sauna.

Just as I thought things could not get any worse, Zara walked in and proceeded to introduce her friend Raoul to a room of silence. Their tiny footsteps could be heard around me as she said, 'And this is my sister . . .' Hidden under the duvet, I stalled my breath for an entirety of ninety-eight seconds as they toured my room looking for me, not realising that whenever they sat on the bed they were crushing a body.

To add insult to injury, I heard a male voice—too high pitched to be Uncle Keith's—nearing the door.

'Come outside, Raoul,' he chirped reminding me of Tweety—my least favourite cartoon, as he was a bird. Oh, God bless anyone with that voice. At this point, the heat felt more intense than ever as I smothered my face further to conceal myself. Now, just because his son was stupid, didn't mean he was. Oh, how wrong I was. Instead of respecting the privacy of someone's bedroom, he proceeded to join the children and sit on top of the bed unaware he was committing a murder. Okay it was going to be difficult to make it. Suddenly, my innovative mind conceptualised a way to run away from the hounds of hell that had been chasing me my entire life and were now finally about to find the one they had always lusted after. I could barely catch a breath. It was time to be creative—the coffin pose. I crossed my hands over my chest and closed my eyes preparing to be spiritually transported. On Sunday, I would come back to life like Jesus, for I would haunt my mother until she took back the fact my face looked like a jellybean.

Eventually, Raoul, his father and Zara decided to stand up unaware of the soul resting in peace beneath them. Hiding under the duvet just wasn't normal—it made zero sense, as there was the additional hazard of life suction. Hiding behind the curtain was a much better idea—it even provided me with a fine view of the street so I could integrate with society. It's what I usually did, so I have no idea what made me choose the bed this time. At least, I knew to avoid that place in the future.

Whilst hiding behind the curtain again, I looked out of the window and saw two children, one giant, two women dressed identically, and one bald man—I recognised Aunty Jazz, Uncle Keith, and Zara with the other family.

Don't fret too much about your troubles—they'll be out of the window before you know it.

Chapter 11

Poga

We're often warned not to overstay our welcome in conversation, but an occasional lapse to the rule reminds us not to follow convention.

A very interesting group of creatures, for I'm not too sure what species they were, came to visit us for dinner one night. When we were informed that a guest and his family were coming over for dinner, we prepared ourselves for the mandatory awkward silences and limited conversation that often accompany a meal with those whom one is not acquainted. My grandfather informed us that his longtime buddy—a famous, high profile owner of a chain of seven star hotels worldwide—was arriving, in tow with his two sons and his wife, thus providing a wide age range appealing to the majority of our family rather than an elitist few.

The minute they walked through the door, they prepared us for an unconventional night. Now most families who visit us at least put on the pretence of being vaguely functional apart from once when extremely distant relatives (so distant, we did not know how they were exactly related) of my grandfather visited and the men and women segregated themselves to dine separately. However, what was fascinating about RD Maskerenas and his family was their attempt to seem like they had it all put together, which they gave up on ten minutes into their arrival. What none of us could also comprehend was their gene pool. When they walked through the door, I saw an Indian husband, a much younger Moroccan wife who looked nineteen, a North African man who appeared to be in his twenties, and an olive-skinned teenager. Somehow, they all were related to each other. With nothing much left to be said, the majority of us performed a vanishing act, leaving my grandparents to entertain in the barroom.

Half an hour later, I emerged into what looked like an ad for the United Colours of Benetton, given the multiculturalism of the people in the room. 'Very nice to meet you,' said the mother in a thick accent and friendly tone despite the lack of emotion on her face. Her pursed lips and arched eyebrows told the tale of a past cosmetic surgery, leaving her looking permanently perplexed. Over the course of the evening, it became clear that the two men accompanying them were indeed their sons. Strangely, the wife whose name we still do not know, kept saying 'Poga' throughout the conversation. I wondered why she kept making such a strange sound until we realised that that was their elder son's name—the only one of the two to whom we were introduced, as the younger one religiously maintained a vow of silence. It was only when we were all standing near the dining table that Poga's sheer mass hit us like a storm. He made my 6'2" uncle who was a quintal at the time appear undernourished. At least four inches taller and built like a box, Poga overwhelmed not just the room, but also the bungalow.

'Can I sit on the hammock? I'm afraid it won't take my weight?' he asked.

'You can try,' said my mother. As we settled at the table with my grandfather and RD visibly inebriated, my grandfather narrated the story of the creation of God.

'Madam,' he droned as we listened to the most haphazard, hastily edited rendition of the bible. It was almost like watching Taken 3 again—a franchise which the makers deliberately worsened over time so that we begged them to stop.

At the table, as Poga took a while to get used to sitting so low—a normal level for all of us, Uncle Keith offered him the crabs. 'No I'm dieting' was his response to a room of stunned silence.

'What willpower,' Uncle Keith responded aptly. During the meal, RD's wife continually reminded him that they had a flight to catch at 11 p.m. But after a few glasses of wine, this matter seemed to be forgotten.

Strangely, every three minutes, RD and my grandfather patted each other multiple times declaring, 'We're like brothers.'

The frequency of this interestingly increased after RD declared he had married four times, but luckily the great gambler had retired citing, 'I can't see at night.' While Poga had made his presence felt with every step taken, the younger son who I'm quite sure was picked up on their travels through the Mediterranean, was far more out of place in the family breathing two sentences.

Ten minutes later, as I was on my way downstairs, I heard a hush and a thud as the Moroccan wife stamped Poga's foot (I'm sure it barely made a mark given his thick padding) with her stiletto. I have no idea what language an African and a Moroccan would converse in, but if it happens to be Zulu, then that would make sense. They appeared to be having an incomprehensible tiff on the stairs. I had never been so voyeuristically entertained since I'd watched the Wolf of Wall Street, and thoroughly enjoyed my bird's eye view until Poga craftily peered up the spiral of stairs. I shot myself back against the wall congratulating myself for extreme subtlety. But didn't they know walls had ears, especially those in a household with many people?

It was now 2 a.m.—nobody knew about the status of their impending flight, but by the end of the evening many were praying for them to get on it.

Nonetheless, Poga has made a special place in all our hearts following revelations of his vegan diet and sheer personality. When on holiday in the Maldives for my birthday one year later, the hotel staff had placed a bouquet of flowers outside my door. Oblivious to this, I asked who placed it there—instantaneously, the response from my family was 'Poga'. Heaven forbid.

'Forbidden' love appears to be most fascinating judging by the history of my family.

Chapter 12

Paris

Many know Audrey Hepburn once said, 'Paris is always a good idea'. What many don't know was that she was inebriated.

I had first visited Paris on a trip to Disneyland as a three-year-old. Thirteen years later, I was finally visiting again having heard friends rave about the fashion, food, and panache of the city. People say 13 is an unlucky number; however, I view it as my lucky one. In this case, for the first time, people were 100 per cent correct. Most of our family friends who had visited once just couldn't stop after that. There was something about the place that had the power to catch hold of a stranger and never let them go—even the most proper would pick up a French accent at the airport and sit at an outdoor café eating croissants thinking they were the daughter Coco Chanel never had.

Fortunately, I am. And so much like Coco, I only wear black and can only be myself much like the rest of my family; although I am incredibly amenable as chameleon—flexibility is key to survival. But our long held values and traditions prevent us from joining a nouveau riche gang who believe they are Parisian and all else is Primark the minute they walk down Champs-Élysées. I have absolutely nothing against the French—they are a wonderful people with a praiseworthy aesthetic and proficiency for the finer things in life—I just strongly believe that this worldwide image of them created by intoxicated tourists as the dictators of taste and style is skewed, given the contribution of every culture to a sense of global aesthetic. This perception of mine was strengthened following my visit there.

Having arrived on the Eurostar, we (my mother, Sid, Aunty Jasmine, Zara, and I) caught a taxi oblivious to the fact that the driver was going to metaphorically take us for a ride. At the end of the ten-minute journey, he announced the cost to be 100 Euros. Visibly shaken but not wanting to create a riot given we were still new arrivals, my mother reluctantly handed over the money as we proceeded to the Ritz. Looking forward to a luxurious stay, the man not bearing a smile, listened as Aunty Jasmine gave our details. Shocked to find that we were not booked in—a major oversight on my mother's part—she appears to be having more of these as she gets older. We walked onto the middle of the road as our heads darted from one corner to the other like lost dogs. It was only a three-day trip and a Holiday Inn could be spotted from afar—we permanently distrusted taxis following our earlier harrowing experience. Having arrived at Holiday Inn, we were in for many more wonderful surprises. At least, the receptionist was friendly and readily gave us a suite claiming the hotel was not fully booked. In hindsight it is not surprising why, but at the time it seemed like a dream.

'How far away is the station from here?' my aunt asked.

'A two-minute walk,' he responded. Having inferred the taxi driver was decent enough to take us in circles so that his fee appeared justified (barely though), I had a newfound respect for the locals' desire to put on a performance. Paris really was the centre of arts.

With our three suitcases, we made our way towards the lift to find a sign that read 'permanently broken', implying it will never be fixed, so basically we had checked into hell. Holiday Inn also lacked any porters as we physically dragged our luggage up four flights of stairs. Once we opened the doors to our suite, we were greeted by the smell of cigarette smoke and the view of a man in the opposite building whose feet were permanently hanging outside the window. The good news is, we didn't do the same. Though losing our minds would be justified.

Of course, I can't be entirely cynical about the trip given the wonderful food, which I wasn't able to eat being a vegetarian at the time. There's only so long Stilton and bread can satisfy you, and I learnt the French, much like the Thai, have a common distaste for green eating. At a restaurant, having explained my situation, they promptly provided me with a prawn salad.

'It's a vegetarian prawn,' the waiter said.

'The prawn was a vegetarian?' I asked. I had never felt so lost in my life.

Despite having learnt French and understanding it fluently for roughly thirteen years, there really is no point conversing with Parisians in their home language unless you're using it to hash tag pretentious phrases on Instagram. If you've not felt like an outsider, you certainly will when talking to them. Paris is a place people discover by foot, as every corner breathes art. So naturally, the most common thing you will find yourself doing is asking a local for directions. While looking for the Galeries Lafayette, I asked a woman slowly in English, 'Excuse me, please could you tell me how to get here?'

To which she responded in the same language, 'I'm sorry I don't speak English.'

So 'if you can't beat them, join them' is the popular adage and whilst I've never been in the crowd, this time I had no option but to join and it, of course, backfired. I walked up to a woman starting a sentence in French. With the kind of look she gave me midway, I just wanted to pick up her hand and slap myself for even trying.

Her reaction was, 'Are you speaking in English or French?' At least she spoke English.

Of course, as usual, we were in a loop of cyclical difficulty so when we realised this, getting to know the 'locals approach' was like knocking on someone's door and never being answered as you watch them from the window, sitting in their living room enjoying a cricket match—we were compelled to turn to the taxi drivers we had previously shunned. The driver in Paris turned out to be more judgemental than the locals who refused to help, as he insulted us in a way never done before. When in the taxi, whilst driving down the Champs-Élysées, we were trying to find a restaurant for dinner. Whilst scouring appropriate bistros and questioning about how good they were, we suddenly passed a well-lit, glass building that looked very impressive. When asking if we could stop there, our driver suddenly pointed and shouted, 'No, that's too expensive for you! Sarkozy goes there.' Oh why didn't God deafen me before making my ears bleed in such a way! I felt like banging him on the head with my Galeries Lafayette bags (more of a victory badge having finally found the building). Pierre has been blacklisted ever since for his inability to make accurate inferences.

When you feel unwelcomed in a place you had looked forward to visiting, the most comforting feeling is to find home lurking at 10 p.m. in a street alley. And so we found Rama's—an Indian restaurant—a reassurance to my homegrown, simpleton brother who was missing his roots. Of course, upon walking in to take away for Sid, the entirely French staff's first reaction was, 'We don't speak Indian.'

Being lost in translation is a state of limbo no one wants to go through the torture of being suspended in.

Chapter 13

Violin

When a child learns music, families join in the atmosphere of rejoicing. But when I open my mouth, my mother says she hears vessels crashing.

I speak on behalf of a sizeable portion of humanity when I say that most of us have been forced to pursue some kind of activity, pastime, and maybe even, profession. Luckily, I hail from a family where my aunt and my mother have not put any pressure on Zara, Sid, or me to follow a particular line, or do something for them. From a young age, only a few aspects have been expected out of us: to be good human beings (work in progress), to give back to society, and to work hard—everything else is either not in our control, or an individual choice we have the freedom to make. Unfortunately, the idea of hard work has been skewed to sometimes only refer to what we view as real life or in the workplace. But for us, preparing and instilling the qualities of ambition and hard work start at the very foundation level in school.

Hailing from an extremely educated family where most members have more than at least one Masters, school is seen as important as a full-time job. But at the same time, I also come from a family that sees the world with a pragmatic view. My grandfather, being self-made albeit at a very young age, values the school of life above any other. His lessons have taught us that topping every subject does by no means equate into succeeding in life. That's probably why I don't feel the shame most students feel sitting in a class, not understanding anything. Because everybody has their own field, much like the rest of my family, I will find mine organically.

Nonetheless, when I was six, my mother suggested I start playing a musical instrument. I was actually excited at the prospect and chose the violin as my most preferred option. I then tried the guitar, the drums (to vent my angst), musical theory, and it turned out the violin was still my most preferred option. Looking back, I think the harp only played by two students in London would have placed me in the group I am most comfortable in—the minority. Having sat at numerous birthday parties (I'm past the age of having them, but with a 7-year-old cousin), I've observed the brightest coloured sweets often taste the most sour, even repulsive. My experience with the violin was somewhat similar.

Everything has an expiry date, but I have a disease where no matter how much I struggle, I have to complete the task even if it exhausts me. The violin wasn't powerful enough to exhaust me. But it gave me the power to not only stick it out through circumstances that were difficult, but also convert them into successes. I started on a roll touted by my teacher to reach Grade 5 within three years, which was a fairly decent time in which to achieve the feat. Three years later in my last few years of primary school, I found myself with a teacher who suspiciously smelt of whisky during our 9.30 a.m. lessons, which I thought to be her fetish for wearing her husband's cologne, but later turned out to really be whisky.

Then eventually hitting an all-time low upon my entry into high school, I found myself being taught by the female version of Alec Baldwin's character from friends. I appreciate optimism and showing one the light at the end of the tunnel, but if you're sinking at the bottom of an ocean and don't know how to swim, then there's no point showing one false hope of reaching the top. Nonetheless, even if my playing sounded worse than fingernails scratching a blackboard, she would say, 'Let's just try a little less so fantastically shrill.' But she padded up the balloon of my ego to such an extent I desperately felt the need to prick it with a pin and give myself a reality check.

Every three months, she would ask me about the status of my brother's playing who himself was nothing short of a musical genius. Despite having started playing five years after me, he was nearing the same level—Grade 3. What also didn't make me look any better was that whilst he had been learning for two years, I had been learning for seven.

'Oh no, we must not let him catch up with you,' she would say in good humour. A while after when she enquired, I explained that he had just given his exam, the same one I had been preparing for the past three and a half years. 'Oh, don't worry. We'll be done with this soon and you both will be on the same level.' When six months later she asked the standard question, I explained that he had skipped Grade 4 and gone straight to Grade 5, which he was due to give in a couple of months.

'Oh,' was her quiet response. 'Let's start playing the piece,' she said urging me to play the same piece of music I had been preparing for the past four years for my never occurring exam. 'Fantastic, fantastic!' she would say, cutting me halfway clapping her hands before goading me on to the next. But then, to be fair to her, she probably couldn't bear listening to the end so this was the only way of stopping the torture.

Having practised for three months religiously before the exam, unlike many others including my own brother, I actually valued the fact that I was being given the opportunity to showcase all my years of hard work continuously going at the same pace for the past four years. The fact that someone so important from a royal music academy was spending their Saturday morning to come to listen to someone as untalented as myself, made the whole episode even more exciting. Having actually done two of these exams before in primary school, I'd learned that unlike a lot of other assessments, in this case, the nicer the examiner, the higher the grade you were likely to be given. Well if this was a game of gaining sympathy, this wasn't going to be a problem for me.

Before stepping into the room, I prepared myself to win over the examiner's heart. This was going to be easy. If not, then he could at least view me as a charity case. Either way, as long as I could pass and get this over and done with (not an attitude I adopt for many situations, but for this one, it was 110 per cent justified). I walked in remembering the importance of endearing myself to the examiner. I wanted to smile and bear all my pearly whites. But then, remembering that I hadn't worn my braces for two days, I ditched the plan and instead showcased my closed mouth smile for strangers at the time. He looked scared, but if that was going to work in my favour, then I would happily continue doing so. He asked me to play my pieces during which in the middle of one he suddenly closed his eyes and shook his head back as if he'd received an electric shock. This became a common occurrence worrying me slightly, but I continued playing regardless. If he could get his fits later, that would be great. Then again, if that meant he couldn't hear my playing because he'd entered a bad place, I was also okay with that. Wow, things were really going well for me.

After I had finished torturing him with the sound of my playing, he sweetly clapped and then suddenly proceeded to the piano in the corner of the musical room. 'Okay, I'm going to play some notes so you can sing them back to me.'

When did singing become a part of the exam? My voice has sounded like a man's since birth; hence, whenever my brother or I call out to our mother from a corner in the house, she understandably can never distinguish between the two of us.

'La lalala,' I said all in the exact same pitch and note—the lowest one available on the chart. He distorted his eyes into a funny shape; squinting them and flared his nostrils—his face looked as if somebody had forcibly shone a bright light on it.

'Okay, now I'm going to play you a piece of music so that you can describe it to me in three words.' This was my chance to score finally as he had indirectly asked me how good my English was to which we all knew the answer. Before he'd played his 30-second piece, I'd already made up my mind what words I'd use.

'Mellifluous, bounteous, and euphonious,' I said with a serene smile. Finally, an eyebrow was raised, as he was visibly impressed. Now was the time to bare teeth. I flashed my whites recognising I'd just hit it out of the park waiting for the next question.

'Thank you very much the exam is over,' he said, looking understandably relieved. That went by rather quickly. Now was the time for me to make small talk and win him over.

'Have a nice weekend. Goodbye,' I said awkwardly.

As I walked down the stairs to find my violin teacher prepping the next candidate for the exam, she turned with an overtly concerned expression on her face. 'How was it?'

'I think it was fine,' I responded. Of course, she followed this with a torrent of praise and congratulations for a certificate that may not even be awarded in a month's time. The truth is, I really didn't know how it went. I walked back to the same room my violin teacher was rehearsing in with another student. 'Actually I don't really think . . .'

'No, no just go home,' she asserted.

'But I really don't . . .'

This time pushing me literally out of the door, she exclaimed, 'Go home! Have a party! Just have a party!'

The student from inside joined in, 'Just have a party!'

I don't know if they had been drinking whilst I was up there, but if I could bear myself playing for the past seven years, then the examiner definitely could for twenty minutes. Two months later, the post carried good news. I not only had passed my violin exam but had also scored a whole mark more than my brother, when he took the exam two years ago.

I still don't know whom the joke was on.

Chapter 14

Catherine

The question that tells me the most about people when I first meet them is—'Are you a dog person, or a cat person, or both?'

'Why would she do this when she already has so many things piled up?' my mother asked conveying both her inability to comprehend and her amusement at the situation. Laughing at the hilarity of our own bad luck/self-destruction, and maybe even fondness to cut our own golden goose, is our family tradition. It's funny because everyone sees the silver spoon we were born with, but they forget that to the person even the brightest cutlery can appear no less than a wooden ladle when neither having our cake, nor eating it too.

'Madam started crying when she saw it'. She told us, 'Put it in a bucket and take it to Sharma (the local vet who is responsible for sending our dogs to their early graves),' said Sharon, Zara's nanny. My mother laughed her usual smile—exasperated at the people surrounding her, yet it was always a genuine one—she only laughed when she found something genuinely worth it. Although investing in what truly deserves such commitment, humour aside, seems to be an inability in our family as far as people go. This entire semi-soap drama is referring to an injured kitten found outside my aunt's home having been cruelly trampled over by a very knowing passer-by. I am humane, along with being human, believe it or not, and have always been an animal lover. When I was five years old, adults resorted to those clichéd questions most commonly asked, 'What do you want to be when you're older?'

Of course, friends of mine would prematurely respond, 'doctor', 'policewoman', maybe even 'lawyer' if their parents were one.

But I was never a slave to my species or a part of the GG (generic gang) as I responded, 'a dog'.

Naturally, both my mother and I were concerned about the kitten, and more about my aunt who was in the middle of umpteen issues—including firing a loyal aide to my grandfather, organising Zara's birthday party, and arranging for a driver with a cold to visit the doctor, and had willingly and absolutely admirably increased the intensity of her ever growing migraine. So we periodically rang up, concerned about her well being as she reported her anxiety regarding the kitten. The good news was, it was still battling for its life.

'She's a fighter,' my aunt had animatedly expressed whilst ironically sprawled across the sofa in the barroom falling out of her trademark floral maxi. So this kitten, trampled over, with a broken leg, but still making its way with convoluted difficult breathing, resonated with my aunt, my mother, and I. It's important not only to be a fighter but also a survivor.

Zara woke up from one of her few naps that provided the house with a much-needed break. Her first question was of course, about the cat. Realising we were useless, she immediately dialled my aunt's number to get a clearer, more accurate picture of the kitten's well being. You see, it's a rule in our family—it doesn't matter if you are at work, in a meeting, or driving—if your child is calling you, answer the phone—it's a value we brought our mothers up with. Of course, Zara was naturally most interested in—as a 7-year-old already comfortable with pets having grown up with two dogs—was whether they could keep the kitten. My aunt needed to do some quick thinking to avoid a potential hurricane of emotions. My mother and I inched closer towards the phone, perhaps even secretly hoping for one of those rare fights in which we could act as spectators rather than participants. Luckily, as we had actually hoped for, there was nothing of the sort as Zara hung up with a grin.

'So what did she say?' I asked amazed at the sea of calm surrounding her that was usually tempestuous.

'She said the cat's mother will most likely come to the hospital in which case we obviously can't take her home. But if no one comes, then we can keep her,' she replied with a twinkle in her eyes.

Later that evening, after my aunt's daily glasses of diet coke topped with rum, a look was glanced towards my brother at the other end watching his cricket. Pot shots are continually taken in good humour at his gullibility and foolishness at the age of 13, especially when compared to the overwhelming beacon of knowledge superfluously transmitted by my 7-year-old cousin—the result of being the daughter of a 'Battle Hymns of a tiger mother' fan. 'Oh yes, Aunty Jasmine, how's the cat doing?' he called out across the palatial room.

Now, not only did Sid eat whatever he was served, he bought whatever he heard. But he was not innocent—blurting out Santa wasn't actually real and other seemingly small white lies had in the past led to vicious fights transpiring between Zara and Aunty Jasmine, Zara and Uncle Keith, my mother and I. The best advice given to him was to shut up and not believe anything he heard, given his love for half-baked information that could cause nothing less than forest fires in the family as he sat from the side-lines and watched. As a result, I often refer to him as the 'paid audience' of the family, much to his annoyance. So basically, to avoid my cousin finding out the reality that the kitten was unlikely to make it, my mother and aunt wisely decided to go with the same story they told Zara.

'So where's the cat's mother now?' he asked, having bought the entire explanation.

'She's on her way—she called the hospital,' I said. 'She's stuck in traffic though. Hopefully she'll make it in time if she drives fast.'

'Ah, that's good,' he responded happily.

For some, ignorance is bliss, but unfortunately, I will never be given a ticket to this paradise.

Chapter 15

Sri Lanka

Knocking on your neighbour's door makes you appreciate your own home a lot more.

Another interesting holiday has to be the one taken in Sri Lanka during the Christmas of 2010. It was close to home; we could easily make it back in time for the New Year. If we had a good time, it would be a sweet and short trip. And if we didn't, the torture would be over soon. So we were to spend Christmas in Colombo.

We arrived in the city and were on that trademark car journey to the hotel where you stare outside the window and soak in the sights of your surroundings. A hoarding publicised snorkelling, not that any of us could swim, but we were still rather kicked by it. Another billboard advertised skydiving off the top of a mountain. It was a great way to see the back of Sid. When we reached the hotel, Aunty Jasmine asked the reception for a list of the 'Top 10 things to do in Colombo' so that we could maximise the enjoyment in the coming couple of days. They kindly sent up a brochure that also included the number of hours to visit any of these sites. Six hours, eight hours, full day trip . . . it turned out if we wished to do anything apart from laze on the beach, which was unlikely given our perpetual fear of getting a tan, then we were in the wrong part of Sri Lanka. Kandy and other towns that were many hours away, held the key to tourist attractions in terms of wildlife sanctuaries and other leisure activities.

Having been punched in the face with this blow, we sat down for a few minutes, deciding how we would spend the next couple of days without tearing our hair out. It turned out there was a shopping mall nearby, so we proceeded there only to find everything we had been avoiding all our lives, including a famous American restaurant where I had gotten my last allergy having eaten a walnut and vegetable burger in their Singapore branch. Figuring out that this was probably the first mall in the world that could not keep us occupied for even half an hour, we decided to make another plan of action.

My grandmother was adamant on buying some of Sri Lanka's infamous china so we headed off to the 'Tea Rooms', a quaint outdoors style café accompanied by a store selling the country's finest crockery. It was a wonderful experience sitting on the peaceful green lawn sipping tea. As a family, we weren't used to silence. But then, after two hours, it really does hurt your ears. Commotion had to occur, else we didn't feel normal. Anyway, my mother had passed out in the car given how unused she was to such stillness. Zara and I were sent inside to urge my grandmother to hurry up with her shopping, as well as subtly reminding her that this wasn't the place to bargain, namedrop, and flash cash.

Soon, we were whisked in the SUV as the waiters in the cafe peered inside slightly worried about my mother who was still in a deep sleep with her head thrown back. The next day we returned again with no other option of anywhere else to go. History has a habit of occasionally repeating itself and in this case, the calm atmosphere was enough to once again lull my mother into catching some winks. The same waiters stared again in fear at the same woman who now passed out again in the car with the same people. I'm quite sure they thought we drugged her.

Having had enough of the tearooms—it just wasn't meant for people like us. We decided on actually doing something the next day, which happened to be our last in Sri Lanka. Aunty Jasmine, my mother, Sid, Zara, and I decided to visit the Pinnawala elephant sanctuary in Kandy. It didn't matter that it was four hours away. For now, we simply wished to have something to remember Sri Lanka by, anything apart from tea which none of us were avid fans of anyway. The only beverages we liked were in our bar at home. As we set out for the elephant sanctuary the next day, our driver—incidentally named Don—started asking rather personal questions such as our phone numbers, where we lived, our address in Mumbai, our address in London . . . Given that we had two hours left to go and another four-hour drive back to the hotel, we had no choice but to provide fake details which we are pros at doing by now, and actually strangely enjoy.

The sanctuary was an incredible experience as Don led us to the foot of a river where two hundred elephants were playing up close and personal. It was a surreal visual out of a documentary. Suddenly, one of the elephants started shifting a bit as another lifted its trunk. What seemed like a playful fight was actually just a fight. Very soon, we were on our feet escaping the premises we had taken a four-hour drive to as we even saw a few elephants roaming wild on the streets. Don gave us the keys, frightening us at first, as it seemed he was suggesting we drive back ourselves. He said he would join us in a few minutes. We sat safely with the doors locked, not that that would make a difference if an elephant had sat on the vehicle. We waited till Don finally emerged with his trademark bowler hat and dark glasses. We had never seen the man behind the shades. He settled in the driver's seat and handed over a package to my aunt.

'What is this?' she asked, eagerly waiting for him to start the car and drive out of this park where nature roams incredibly close to man.

'Dung paper,' he replied. 'A traditional Sri Lankan gift for you.'

'Thank you' my aunt responded before silently placing the package in the trunk never to pick it up again.

Having reached the hotel after our four-hour drive in which we all, including maybe even Don himself fell asleep, our driver began to question us.

'So when are you leaving tomorrow? What time? I'll be here in the morning.'

My aunt brushed aside any attempts to drive us to the airport that would probably end with being locked in a windowless van. The next day, on returning from the local coffee shop, my grandmother informed us that Don had called. What was even more worrying was that she had taken his number and arranged to send him a box of cashews once we reached Mumbai since he was a big fan of nuts. No wonder he grew so fond of my grandmother.

Sitting in the lounge of the airport, my grandmother asked my aunt whether she had bought any souvenirs, apart from the dung paper left behind. 'Yes' was Aunty Jasmine's dry response. She had bought three identical magnets with a picture of the Pinnawala elephant sanctuary and the words saying, 'I love Sri Lanka'.

The best place to forgive and forget is in the duty-free shop of an airport. Everyone ends up being a winner.

Chapter 16

Nurse

Getting physical is something two parties may be forced to engage in, even if neither of them wishes to.

I first met my school nurse when I was 12. During that meeting, a basic eye test, height measurement, and noting of weight ensued. It was nothing extremely technical or complicated. Finally, I received an email, three years later stating the nurse had been fired, and since I required a recent medical examination to be conducted for a summer school I wished to go on, a visit to my GP was necessary. When I reached the Rosemary Clinic, the receptionist said, 'Dr Kate Brown is not in today. You have a replacement doctor.' Totally oblivious to the fact that it would turn out to be one of those meetings in which I want to beat the cushions and scream for me to be let out the door, I waited in blissful ignorance for my name to be called. It was the middle of June, but I never let go of what I was most comfortable in—my puffy Moncler jacket, velour sweatpants, trainers, and my backpack. I looked like I had just come from an excursion in the Arctic.

As a woman led me to the room, I knocked on the door. 'Come in,' the doctor said. That was strange—her voice was awfully deep, almost like mine.

He didn't even stare at my strange attire once, making me wonder if he also had the same issues as me. 'We'll just be doing a few physical examinations.' Oh dear, this was going to be a problem. He sat at the desk going through the files, trying to find my medical record. At this point, I noticed he had amazingly full lips, and I was dying to ask him what his secret was. Was he born like that, or did he pray to god and they were miraculously thickened, as was the case with myself at the time? I loved hearing about wonder blunders.

'So I see you're allergic to nuts, you've never had to use the Epipen have you?' I shook my head, not wanting to reveal my thin lips in comparison to his if I separated them to create speech. 'Okay, now let's check your heartbeat.' I have to thank god that he wasn't my type, otherwise, this test would have revealed a lot. Being the conscious creature I am, I flinched when I saw the stethoscope as I thought he would just take my pulse at the back of my wrist. Now this was getting a bit racy. I pretended as if I could not hear or see him when he stood up in front of me. 'Excuse me . . . excuse me,' he said, as I stared into his eyes trying to make him uncomfortable. Something I do whenever the opposite person is making me feel that way. 'Sorry I just have to,' he said exasperated as he stuck the stethoscope on me and looked away visibly more tortured than I was.

After that intimate moment of sensing each other's heartbeat, it was time for me to reveal secret information so that the 'weight' section could be filled in. It was essential this was accurate so I took off my shoes, given the amount of weight Nike trainers would add. I stood on the scale realising that my feet were too close together concentrating the weight, which would give an inflated number. So I separated them; in doing so, I jumped by accident causing the scale to flip over at which point the doctor did not even flinch perhaps expecting disaster. Oh, this was ridiculous! I am not 54 kilos. I took off my jacket and tied my hair so that its weight would not be confused with my body. In the midst of this, my hair tie got slightly stuck as I felt the stress of him watching me, and what should have been a two-second job took visibly much longer. I fumbled around with my fingers as a shower of strands fell around me until it was finally held back; 53.8 kilos was much more accurate.

'Okay now your height,' he said as he at this point clutched the top of my skull with his fingers and dragged me towards the measuring pole. He flung me towards it and casually read 5'4".

'That's not possible. I'm 5'5" and a half. It's on my record,' I said visibly worried.

'Oh dear, you must be shrinking', he responded not bothering to measure again. He then proceeded to simultaneously graph my height and weight and compare them with national statistics.

'Are you worried by either of these?' he asked. I told him my weight sometimes bothered me but it was by no means a serious concern. Having performed some mathematical comparison with the average person's statistics, he said that I actually weighed less for my height. Finally, some good news.

'So I'm underweight?' I asked revealing half of my teeth in a sly smile.

'No, you're definitely not underweight' was his immediate response. He just didn't want to give me one reason to go to bed happy.

The eye check-up was next, of which I now know he did a praiseworthy job given that four months later, the opticians assigned me with a power of 1.5 and a pair of frames whilst Rambo (he looked like a Rambo) claimed all was fine. I was suspicious by how half-heartedly it seemed like he was doing things, so when the time came to read letters from afar I deliberately misread some to see what he said. Surprisingly, he congratulated me and said, 'excellent vision.' When examining my throat with a torch, he asked with a lilt in his voice, 'Have you always been asymmetrical?' This set me off on a lifelong path of self-consciousness about my right eye being bigger than my left, and my face looking like it was made using one of the distorting features on photo booth. I take back all the praise I showered on his lips.

Since then, to avoid any chance meeting with the doctor, I've treated all illnesses that have unfortunately arisen myself at home. That's why I'm still suffering.

Chapter 17

Spanish

I've never met myself because there are so many of me to meet.

Having been fortunate enough to have studied in a private, leading school in London, the abundance of languages that were available on offer was mind-blowing. But I still was prey to my 'thaasophobia', otherwise known as a fear of being bored. So in order to further keep myself busy, I told my mother I wanted to learn Spanish outside of school. Always being one to support me, she immediately signed me up the next day at the Spanish Institute in Belgravia, which entailed a fifteen-minute drive. The next day, when I arrived from school, she let me know that the class would take place every Saturday from 2 p.m. to 5 p.m. She was worried if this would ruin the chance of me making weekend plans. Honestly, if such a thing existed that I could ruin, I would be thrilled, but I had to be realistic. What my mother also forgot to mention was that this was a strictly adults class which had no place for a 16-year-old.

I walked into the Spanish Institute, which appeared totally empty, and asked which floor the classroom was on. They obviously refused to speak English, but they wouldn't let me go until they were sure I understood what they had said. I finally nodded and said, 'Yes okay.'

Of course, I had absolutely no idea and so climbed all ten flight of stairs to check inside the twenty classrooms on each floor. I was too awkward to knock and walk in like a generic person would, so I would place my ear to the door to listen out for breathing and other signs of human life on the other side. In every case, I would invariably hear silence. The whole building could not have been evacuated and unless this class was taking place in the washroom, my ears were obviously failing me. So I climbed down all ten flights of stairs to go to the reception and ask which floor it was on.

'I just told you . . . top floor', came the harsh response. But it was fine because if I fainted halfway, she would have to carry me. They couldn't just trample over a corpse. Finally, I heard some voices—at least thirty people followed by an elderly man walked in, holding Starbucks coffees. I followed them up the stairs in case they were in the very class I had hoped to join. Somehow, already knowing where the classroom was, they didn't feel the need to ask the receptionist what floor it was on.

In a few seconds, I had found myself close on the heels of the couple who I'm hoping were married, for if not, their spouses definitely had something to be worried about. At this point, the lady turned behind and smiled at me. Being the way I am, I turned my head away to the right and found a corner on the wall and stared at it. For some reason, she kept looking at me.

At this point, I took a side flick of my hair and hung it like a curtain to conceal a side of my face whilst I picked up my phone on the other and called my mother—'Tell the driver to come early. My class will finish at 5.' The driver was my mother. By then, they had gone ahead but she continually passed me pleasant looks though I sensed she'd figured I was a strange person. What gave it away? Unfortunately, there were still nine flights of steps left—yes, it was on the top floor, which gave me plenty of time to unknowingly catch up with and even overtake the pair. Not a good idea, given I had absolutely no idea where I was going but could not reveal my dependence on them at this point. So being a good thirty steps ahead of them I hid in a corner (my favourite pastime) in the bathroom. Finally, hearing their voices loud and clear again, I realised they must have gone ahead and stepped out only to find them still lagging behind. By this time, they had seen me shuffle backwards and forwards as my entire body performed its trademark awkward dance. I pressed some buttons on my phone, transformed my face into a serious expression and said, 'Tell the driver she's fired.'

'What?' my mother asked on the other end. Thank god they had walked ahead. Finally, I followed them into the classroom only to have the end of my Burberry trench get caught on the knob so I was pulled back whilst entering the room. I was born to be noticed, maybe God was trying to tell me this and do me a favour by hampering all my efforts to be discreet given that was a way of living I wasn't born to have.

When finally sitting on a red seat far too small to accommodate a decently fed human being, I stared in surprise at the visibly much older crowd I was left with. It may be more difficult winning over these hearts. The teacher walked in, speaking in Spanish from the minute she entered, and gave what I suppose was some sort of an uplifting speech given that it opened to much applause. I joined in with a teeth bearing smile nodding as I pretended to be part of this cult.

After this, what I got from her talk was for everyone to go around and introduce themselves and their reasons for learning Spanish. Someone's husband was Spanish, someone's wife was Spanish, someone had Spanish friends (if that was their way of saying they had friends it wasn't very subtle), someone was moving to Spain . . . Through what may have seemed like a minor introductory activity, this group revealed a lot more to me as I had the power to read between the lines. Firstly, they were already acquainted with each other and gotten on well. This made it difficult for someone like me to show them the right direction when they were so comfortable with what was familiar and wrong— their company was like junk food for each other. Secondly, they had a strange sense of humour and would lack the vision to understand mine. 'I'm a doctor,' said one.

'Oh, so can you treat an aching heart,' jibed another. They all joined in roaring laughter together. Yes, definitely not worth winning any hearts here. I wanted to send them on a one-way ticket to Barcelona. It was my turn and having already been outcast, I had nothing to lose. Instead of

Spanish, I treated it like the Drama class I would never take, and took the opportunity to be another person. Still weird like I am, but I would change my name, nationality, address, everything and have my own fun. Somehow these people weren't as foolish as I thought. 'I'm Spanish, but we moved when I was three so I've never learnt the language. This will make me feel closer to my roots.'

'I thought you were Indian,' said the American who had many friends.

'That's funny, I get that a lot.' The temperature in the room was rising as I removed my trench coat and wiped a bead of sweat off my face.

'Which part of Spain are you from?'

'The north' seemed like a safe response. There had to be a north of Spain.

After a stressful introduction to the group, we were told to individually acquaint ourselves with one another by providing bio details. 'Your surname,' somebody asked me. At this point, I needed something Spanish sounding and unfortunately having never known a family from that region I was stuck.

Finally, I got it. 'Ronaldo,' I announced.

'Ronaldo?' the woman asked with an expression of shock at my audacity to lie to her face like this.

'Sorry, do you not know how to spell it?' I asked trying to make her feel foolish. Somehow, this was turned back on me.

Three very long hours were finally over as I waited for everyone else to leave the room, so that I could at least have a peaceful ten-flight walk downstairs. It is only when my driver (mother) arrived that I finally had the chance to blame this whole idea on somebody else and my favourite scapegoat was always her. When I reached home, I also made the important discovery that Cristiano Ronaldo was in fact Portuguese, and not Spanish, as revealed by a quick Google search. What I discovered alongside this was an Armani photo spread I'm not even sorry for viewing. So in the end, as I did with the violin, I maintained my curve of strangeness because I believe in consistency. But I also believe in unpredictability; my condescending peers' willingness to learn may have earned my admiration, but their dismissive attitude of my ability given my age and taking everything on surface value only set me on a fiery path to moving levels above them before they could turn and pat me on the back for mastering 'hello' in Spanish.

They should have known I was an onion; not only did I have many layers, but I could also make them cry. I cannot believe I just said that.

Chapter 18

AI 131

For those that aspire to join the mile-high club, I'd like to recommend flying Air India. There's a chance your plane will never land.

Air India, our government-run airline, has received one feat few airlines today have—the ability to go down in posterity as generations pass on their stories of flying with them. I once heard someone say that the one thing you can be guaranteed on the flight is warm and motherly treatment— warm, because the AC doesn't work, and motherly because the air hostesses are generally above fifty. This is good news for all sauna room fans, as the party never stops when you're up there.

Of late, the airline has been receiving increasing press more than ever before due to their careless crew, poor service, and lack of interest in providing passengers with a relaxed experience in sync with the money paid for a ticket. Their response to mishaps is what has been most bizarre and wonderfully entertaining. When asked about having turned back halfway through a journey to London as a rat was spotted on board, officials said they were investigating the matter.

My mother, Sid, and I travelled Air India until 2010 for all flights from London to Mumbai and vice versa, before the rest of my family knocked the sense into us to switch to the longtime favourite and ever dependable Jet Airways. For some reason, we were once again booked on an AI 131 flight from Mumbai to London, and nothing could have prepared us for what we were in for. Four to six hour delays sound terrible, but we wouldn't have been surprised if that was the case. Nonetheless, that a twenty-four-hour journey would need to be made to go to London was something out of a nightmare I was about to live.

Before boarding, a man walked through the waiting area shouting my name. I was informed my seat was unserviceable and so I would have to move to economy. After justifiably creating a fuss, as clearly the airline hasn't yet understood the concept of compensation, the plane was delayed for twenty minutes. I was the sole passenger to remain in the waiting area as my family carried on. Finally, I was called onto the plane claiming that the problem had been solved. Having reached my seat, I was told it did not recline (the main reason why one would wish to pay extra money and travel business class).

The airhostess said, 'You can eat and drink. The only think you can't do is sleep.' I hadn't arrived for a nine-hour banquet. I wondered how an airline could just so causally inform you that your seat is unserviceable due to their laziness to sort the issue out and prevent you from gaining the perks you pay for as part of a ticket. If I was in economy and my seat was unserviceable would I have to hang off the plane's wing? Eventually, the only steward who helped, agreed to manually push my seat back and so we were ready to take off. I passed out only to wake up to my delight finding out that we had already landed. Except, the truth was, we hadn't taken off for five hours.

Suddenly, an announcement was made in a voice barely in the audible range, (I wonder why?) stating the aircraft had to be changed due to a technical issue. Disgruntled, all passengers were shooed off the plane, leaving us to dream what the status of our flight was and what time it would take off given all Air India staff seemingly went into hiding.

What was most shocking was the sheer unapologetic nature and nonchalance about their lack of organisation that caused such inconvenience—'We're going from bad to worse' was their standard dialogue as if degrading their standards gave them some sort of a sick high. Whilst in the lounge, all members of the business class sat close together so that no one missed out on any kind of information. Finally, we were informed that though the technical snag had been fixed, there was no crew available to service our journey. So we were to board at 5 p.m. (ten hours after the original time. All sent up an immediate prayer to God.

Another interesting shock was that the aircraft, which had a so-called technical problem, had remained unchanged, contrary to what was implied by the original announcement. The good news was my seat had been miraculously fixed (if the ten-hour delay was due to this then I both laud and curse the person who came up with this idea). So it was now time for our earlier crew to pick up their replacements from Delhi—a two-hour flight from where we would take a ten-hour one with our new guardian angels of the galaxy to what would hopefully be our final destination, London. In Delhi, the current crew having completed their clock time could not have gotten off the plane faster. Fearing their lives with the silent banishments to hell received by all passengers, they grabbed all belongings along with some headphones and wine bottles from the cabinet and dashed off.

The new group was quite a cult. If slow and steady wins the race, then they certainly won the title of being the most frustratingly inefficient crew. What also struck everyone somehow telepathically at that moment, was the 11 p.m. curfew at Heathrow airport, for which we were unlikely to make it at that time. Instead of hurrying, our newfound enemies strolled up and down the aisles transferring one possession of theirs each time, be it a facial kit or a pair of glasses. For two hours, this drama went on until the captain could be heard asking in an understandable rage why they weren't ready to take off. Apparently, they hadn't yet found the room spray to fumigate the plane. When have they ever believed in following protocol? Surprisingly, after a two-hour hunt for this air freshener, a lifeless steward, like a body pulled out of the river, bent to the carpeted floor and sprayed it aimlessly at the ground.

When the flight was finally taking off and the safety announcement (seriously, who are we kidding) was made accompanied by its video, we learnt that the aircraft was ironically called the 'Dreamliner.' The intoxicating aroma of pumpkin and mandarin air spray now mixed with the salmon served for dinner by the same steward who had previously refreshed us. At this point, I wished the plane's technical failure had not been fixed so that we could just put a quick end to our misery.

Every cloud has its silver lining. In this case, having been on what felt like a pilgrimage, there was a celebration when we finally landed in Heathrow. Smartly, the air hostess left out translating the Hindi announcement into English, well aware that the arrival time—12.30 would not be pleasing news given Heathrow's curfew. And the airport would be fully justified in making the aircraft wait for five additional hours until flights were officially permitted to land. It appears that not all humanity is missing in the world, and an occasional reminder of this helps you to throw away any cynicism built up by the demons of your mind. Airport officials at Heathrow were more than welcoming and facilitated the entire immigration process.

For once I'd take a leaf out of Nita's book: if you ever find yourself by mistake on an Air India flight booked by somebody who presumably wants to see the back of you—'Expect the worst. It avoids disappointment.'

Chapter 19

Allergy

I've always found it ironic that I, of all people, am allergic to nuts.

It was a tradition of sorts in my class to meet every year for Christmas at one of our homes for dinner. I could never be gracious enough to open the doors of my house and take that kind of responsibility on a Thursday night—I'd leave the dinner halfway to watch the Big Bang Theory and let the guests entertain themselves. Luckily, a wonderful girl Sophia generously offered and we were all to meet at her beautiful home in Chiswick. I was excited for more reasons than one. For as a person, I've struggled with whether I am social or not. I like to believe I was popular and the love I'd received from my school at a school so polarised in opinion has been overwhelming, given my unconventional personality. Take something seemingly small, but actually scarily significant to those who I break the news to—my absence from Facebook. When asked why, I respond, 'Because I have a life.' Another instance when I lie to myself, as well as the opposite person.

So what I'm convolutedly trying to say is that, I was much loved and made sure I had a blast in school with my peers—but outside, work was my priority. So if that meant not stepping out for the year for a wet and wild night of drunkenness until after summer exams, that's what it meant. I got some kind of sick, self-sadistic pleasure when I went to bed at the end of a tiring day and night knowing that I've exhausted my intellectual and creative juices. So basically, after half a term, I was looking forward to seeing people in their natural habitat—a society jungle. Punctuality is not my forte, but a niche sense of style is, as I wore my recently purchased lemon wool sweater from Rag and Bone—a brand my aunt doesn't even know exists, but says it makes sense when I cite it as my favourite store. 'I can't wait; all eyes will be on me,' I said, for I believe in two mottos: 'Honesty is the best policy' and 'Vanity is fair' (my own creation).

'They will all be staring at me. I look great.' I laughed, but meant it seriously.

'Okay,' said my mother. 'You're mad.'

It was 7.30 p.m. and I suffer from direction dyslexia, so navigating my own way to Sophia's house from Chiswick tube station was a nightmare I had already foreseen. Luckily, I eventually found my way thanks to various groups of people who presumably called the police after I'd asked them if they could help me find the address of a young girl. We were warmly greeted and led to the table. I handed over the salmon and cream cheese bagels to her mother who looked exhausted with her tightly tied smock, waiting for the scones to come out of the oven—but she managed a smile which was commendable. Over dinner, we discussed numerous issues although I was occasionally distracted by the sight of a mother who was about to pass out in a corner but the good news is I was told multiple times that I looked lovely.

Do not worry the joke will be on me soon. I enjoyed the multicultural fare consisting of Mediterranean appetizers, spring rolls, and crackers, still unaware of the karma truck that was about to hit me.

Suddenly, my right eye started flickering—a sign my mother considers to be bad luck. I don't really believe in luck as a concept, maybe because I haven't experienced it yet. I do, however, believe in fortune and destiny to which I am both a slave and a puppeteer. In this situation, I was a slave. Soon, my flickering right eye stopped. It had closed to half its size. I kept trying to enlarge my eye and blink, but it was sealed up and I could barely see.

I excused myself to the washroom where an all-too-familiar lump in my throat started forming and my breaths were convoluted and difficult. Of course, I had eaten something with nuts. A concoction of rage, annoyance, desire to laugh at the entire situation, which could only happen to myself, and fear of how to sort this out hit me harder than the overpowering scent of Jo Malone in the bathroom—that too, a sandalwood flavoured eau de toilette. Oh, this really was olfactory hell. Since childhood, I've always been told that I do everything quickly—speaking, thinking, talking, eating, walking, and breathing (I have a deviated septum).

In fact, many times I've been told to slow down and it is times like these that teach me it is more of a gift than a hindrance. Now I could either go up, not say a word and politely wait until the end of the dinner to sort this out at home (which would only be in two hours, provided Sophia's mother didn't pass out anytime soon), or I could go up, explain the situation even if my audience was a little larger than I'd like it to be, and get the help I needed. In hindsight, I definitely made the right choice, which was the latter one. Walking to the station would have been a nightmare as my movements were becoming erratic. Two others ran helter skelter—a couple came to ogle at the animal in the zoo—I had one eye open. There was an unstoppable rash on my nose, and finally, my lips had swollen to the size I'd always wanted them to be.

Sophia's mother had obviously caught wind of the entire situation and walked terrified towards me.

'Did you eat these by any chance?' she asked holding a Marks and Spencer packet with the writing, 'Cheese and Walnut Crackers' printed in large. She didn't need an answer. She took me to the sofa in my half dead state and quietly asked, 'So will you fall ill now, what will happen to you?' The honest answer was I had absolutely no idea and didn't want to know as long as my lips stayed like Angelina Jolie's, and everything else about my face came back to normal, I really didn't want to think about it.

As I sat on that sofa being consistently questioned by Sophia's mother, stared at by a few other peers, unable to speak, see, and walk, I heard a faint sound of celebration in the background. Surely, this wasn't because of my allergy.

'Do you remember the time when she locked herself in bathroom and said the light went off?' asked a friend of mine to a table that opened up into peals of laughter. Even when I'm on my deathbed, people will be laughing and reminiscing in a corner whilst I breathe my last. I don't know whether to be happy about that, or dreading that my demise will be mourned a few minutes later than desired.

So I was packed off in the taxi by an incredibly helpful friend and sent home to a terrified mother who tucked me into bed. She was more than understanding joining me in the cursing of an ignorant member of the group who had brought those crackers, despite having universally decided no nuts would be brought given my allergies. Over the next two days, as I sat at home preparing a speech that would move the crowd—one that involved a diatribe against my allergy bearer, prophetically ending with a praise of the girl who helped me to further deepen the wounds of guilt I would have artfully dug. So I charged from Hammersmith Broadway station ready as the revolutionary that I am to jerk tears, elicit laughter, and finally award my sole friend with the chocolate egg I was carrying as a genuine token of thanks for saving my life and putting me in a taxi. I walked into the room opening my mouth just about to begin my speech, as suddenly one got up to go to the washroom, the other took out her phone, and the third was my saviour.

'Thank you so much for helping me,' I said to her handing over the gift, genuinely meaning it.

'Oh, you really didn't need to,' she sweetly responded. She opened the jar and took one out and then promptly offered one to her neighbour who happened to be the cause of my allergy. My murderer had not only escaped her punishment but was also being indirectly rewarded for attempting to kill me. I was grateful to God for warning me about the future.

The good news was, that evening, all eyes were on me.

Chapter 20

The end of the beginning

Looking at another person often provides a more accurate reflection than looking at a mirror.

We sit at our dining table—the younger generations of the family. My mother and my aunt, along with myself, as Zara prepares for an Olympiad and Sid watches cricket eating his tenth course. My grandparents are probably lying on the lazy boys in their room throwing bones to the dog whose one foot is in his grave.

It is the 30th of December and my aunt has just returned from her trip to the local orphanage where she makes a yearly donation. The significance of it being that it is Zara's birthday, and this place happens to be the vehicle through which she was given to us as Uncle Keith and Aunty Jasmine adopted her from there seven years ago. Apart from this one day in the year, I forget for the remaining 364 that this even happened. I remember years ago how various astrologers who would come home would predict that my aunt would have twin boys. The fact that this did not happen not only saved me the energy of committing two murders, but also served to subtly 'un-teach' some of our preconceived notions and teach us new ones.

I had spent the longest time until the adoption of my cousin going by superstitions—I believed greatly in luck. I always set my right foot outside the door first; I prayed a thousand times for forgiveness if an evil thought entered my head (imagine how many times I would have to do that). I would beat my chest if I saw a black cat crossing the road. I would even believe astrologers who would come home and preach nonsense as charlatans. I wasn't alone in doing this of course; I had learned and imbibed the fear of tomorrow from my family. But we are unconventional. One of us is infatuated with the house help's daughter, the other was sent to a shrink for reasons still being researched, another is adopted, all of us have drinking problems, including the cleaner. In a family like this, how can we ever be afraid or fearing tomorrow when our present unfurls so many exciting facets?

With so many diverse personalities in my family, we somehow don't feel the need to seek approval from anyone else. I've always maintained that I am my own source of criticism and validation—I never need to win a single award in my life and I will still sleep happily if I find my work and lifestyle to be satisfactory, because we, as a unit, have never needed anyone else's approval.

Recently in London, someone told me that I should reflect more. Whilst I appreciate the advice, this person forgot that though I belong to a family that can provide me with everything I could wish for, I also hail from India. All I need to do is to walk down the street there and that's enough of a reminder of my good fortune. That is my motivation to work harder and give back to society, and as my grandfather says, 'Keep the family flag flying.' What this person was also not aware of was my strong grounding. I've heard that Chanayka, the famous Indian philosopher once said, 'He who is overtly attached to his family members experiences fear and sorrow, for the root of all grief is attachment. Thus one should discard attachment to be happy.'

But for me, this sense of attachment anchors me to the ground—it's responsible for imbibing a sense of humility inside of me, and bringing me down to earth. My family has maintained its values from day one, and they've been passed onto generations. We know and understand the transient nature of fame and wealth, and will never take songs of praise or criticism to heart. That's why the idea of giving back to society and understanding all that separates us, and the person knocking on the car window is destiny, is so essential to our core values. The rising sun is always saluted, and we understood that long before many of the other stars on the horizon did. Our vision and ability to see beyond tomorrow is what renders me from having any fear of it, because whatever happens, I know I will be told when I am going in the right direction, and especially when I am going in the wrong one.

Every family unit is different and can be made up of different individuals. There is no perfect model of how a family should look or be, so long as they're together. As long as you have one to be with is all that matters. I have no idea what will happen with my life tomorrow or whether I'll get any of the things I wish for, but somehow, even the worst happening doesn't scare me, not even death, because even if I die tomorrow I've spent time with the people I was meant to be with—no matter how weird they may be.

We make up for one another's shortcomings—if one of us embarrasses ourselves at a dinner, the other will try to outdo the member in that department so that the emotion of wanting to run out of a room screaming is at least shared. We are the way we are, and it's worked for us so far. Celebrate living with mad people if you do, because not everyone is lucky to.

Normal families make more friends; dysfunctional families make more memories.